The Exceptional Child

The Exceptional Child
A Guidebook for Churches and Community Agencies

Edited by
James L. Paul

Syracuse University Press   1983

Library of Congress Cataloging in Publication Data

Main entry under title:

The Exceptional child.

Includes bibliographical references.
1. Handicapped children—Addresses, essays, lectures.
2. Religious education of exceptional children—
Addresses, essays, lectures. 3. Handicapped children—
Services for—Addresses, essays, lectures. I. Paul,
James L.
HV888.E89 1983 362.4'0458'088054 82-16914
ISBN 0-8156-2287-2
ISBN 0-8156-2288-0 (pbk.)

Manufactured in the United States of America

Contents

Preface

SOCIAL RELATIONSHIPS are as important to our psychological development and well-being as food, clothing and shelter are to our physical survival. We work and play and learn in groups. We live in groups. We bring what we have into places where there are other people who bring what they have—abilities, needs, attitudes, physical appearance, and so forth. There are tall people and short people, but height does not make a difference unless one is too tall or too short. There are thin people and people who are obese, but weight does not make a difference unless it is too extreme. There are smart people and people who have more difficulty understanding, but that does not make any difference unless one is too slow to understand and act. Some who come into the group have physical abnormalities or deformities; but that does not make any difference unless it is too extreme. Some are very active and some are very passive, but only excessive aggression or passivity will be a problem. What difference makes a difference? It depends in large part on the values of the people who are present and what is expected in the particular situation.

For the most part differences are of interest but are not a problem. Usually differences are negotiated, and individuals find ways to work and get along together in groups. Sometimes, however, the differences do make a difference, and the individual and the group need help in adjusting to each other. This is often the case when handicapped children are included in the normal activities of everyday life in the community. Children in religious education classes, for example, or recreational and even preschool groups, and other organizations in the community need information so that they can understand and be helped to accept children who are in some way very different from themselves.

The adult leaders in these groups need to know the special needs of exceptional children and how to meet those needs in the context of a normal group of children. Adults sometimes need help with their own feelings about extreme physical and psychological differences. In order to help nonhandicapped children accept the differences in the behavior and/or appearance of handicapped children, the teacher needs to be accepting of these differences and be able to relate to the child and the child's family.

The handicapped child who would participate in normal activities needs help. This child needs to be taught appropriate behavior, when behavior is a problem. The child may need to be taught how to contribute to the activities of the group. It is not unusual for a teacher and a group of nonhandicapped children to have difficulty meeting the special needs of some of these children. A retarded child, for example, can try the patience of a teacher and a group who want to "get on with the lesson." A hyperactive or disruptive child can quickly exhaust a teacher who is trying to manage the child's behavior during an organized activity. A teacher may have debilitating sympathy and fear when presented with the information that a child in the class has a terminal illness. A child in a wheelchair can appear very frail, which may inhibit the teacher's normal interactions with the child: the teacher may keep a distance from the child because of fear. This attitude can set up a situation in which the child feels different and rejected. It may also permit the child to manipulate the teacher, using the handicap and the teacher's fear to get his or her way when the other children cannot. If the child is to be taught and helped to grow socially, emotionally and intellectually, the teacher must operate from a position of strength, knowing his or her own feelings and the needs of the child. The teacher needs to know the child's level of functioning and begin at that level.

The child's family is very much involved in his or her participation in the activities of the community. Parents of handicapped children face many special problems in raising their children. Their children have not had the successes that nonhandicapped children have had, and these parents are often more involved in efforts to find some positive educational experience for their child and to be an advocate for the child as needed.

It is important for ministers, rabbis, priests, religious education and preschool teachers, camp counselors, and other adults in the community who are likely to come in contact with handicapped children and their families to understand their special needs and be able to respond as constructively and helpfully as possible. This book was written to assist in that process. It is written for the nonspecialist in the community, that is, the person without a specific background in psychology, special education, or other academic areas commonly associated with professional services for exceptional children and their families.

This book is written to provide very practical help in understanding and responding to needs. It is written with the religious education teacher in mind who has a child appear for her class and is told, "David has grand mal seizures. I don't believe he will have one during the morning, but if he does I hope you will be able to give him some support." Or perhaps there is a child in her classroom who will not sit still or obey her in any way. It is written with the minister in mind who is counseling with a family considering the issue of institutionalization of their severely retarded child. It is written with the scout leader in mind who is trying to work with a child who has been labeled emotionally disturbed. In a word, this book was written for those who need help understanding and working with children with a wide variety of special needs.

A child is part of a family and a community. He or she depends on resources in these social systems for support. If the child has special needs for support, that is, needs more support and support that is different from that required by most other children, special demands are made on the family and the community.

The community is complex and made up of many components; including the church or synagogue, school, other social agencies, and professional service providers. The services of these different components must be orchestrated so that the child and family receive the services that are needed at the time they are needed. It requires a lot of cooperation among these various components in order to provide continuity of services and avoid unnecessary and costly duplications. There is now a rather large bureaucracy associated with the delivery of human services in the community. It requires a lot of effort by concerned and caring professionals and lay people alike in order for the services of these agencies to be efficiently and effectively provided. There is an important advocacy role for individuals and for institutions that would work to improve the lives and life chances of handicapped children and provide meaningful support to families of handicapped children.

This book includes seven chapters, each of which deals with some specific aspect of the child's life. The first four chapters present information about the needs of exceptional children. The first chapter provides a personal perspective of a parent with years of experience trying to find a meaningful place in the community for her severely retarded son. In Chapter Two the focus shifts to the perspective of professional knowledge available about the specific characteristics and needs of exceptional children. In Chapter Three the family is discussed in terms of its impact on the child and the child's impact on the family. The needs of families are discussed in relation to the changes that take place in the family over time as the handicapped child matures and makes different demands on the emotional, social, and physical resources of the family. The community is discussed in Chapter Four. The emphasis is placed on what is needed by exceptional children and their families, what is available to meet these needs in the community, and how one gets access to these resources.

In all of the first four chapters the discussion of needs of exceptional children and their families and resources available in the community is at a very practical level, with an emphasis on specific needs. The authors have tried to be very careful to communicate clearly in jargon-free language, since the primary audience of this book is the layperson who does not necessarily have a background in one of the helping professions.

In the last three chapters the emphasis on what to do to help and how to do it is even more specific and concrete. In Chapters Five and Six the emphasis is placed on how to work successfully with an exceptional child in a religious education class, for example, or in a scout group. The authors, both experienced teachers, provide specific suggestions about how to handle problematic situations that arise in work with exceptional children.

In the last chapter, discussion focuses specifically on pastoral help for families of handicapped children. Members of the clergy have tremendous opportunities to help handicapped children and their families. Some of this help can be provided directly in the normal activities of the church or synagogue. These activities can range from seeing that teachers are trained and supported in their work with handicapped children, to pastoral counseling for the family. They include seeing that the physically handicapped have access to the sanctuary, the educational facilities, and the bathrooms. They include seeking to have the appropriate educational equipment available for the partially sighted, for example, and seeing to it that the hearing impaired can participate in the services of worship. Here, in the center of the religious life of a community, are many opportunities for ministry and for outreach activities to help bring about a larger caring community for the handicapped. Specific suggestions for ways to do this are contained in Chapter Seven.

Practical guidance for the nonprofessional is emphasized throughout this book. It is important, however, to recognize that there is not a "cookbook" for caring. Concern about the special needs of vulnerable children and their families and the motivation to become involved in ways that will be helpful and reduce their vulnerability are highly individual matters. The practical guidance in this book begins with the assumption that one cares and wants to help and needs to understand how to go about it.

A final note should be made about what to call these "special children." The question of how to refer to people with disabilities is an important one. As William Cruickshank points out in Chapter Two, language is a powerful conveyor of attitudes, and the professionals who work with handicapped persons are continuously looking for language that is free of the negative connotations that often accompanied terminology formerly in common use. But the question of how to refer to people with disabilities is far from settled, as the reader of this volume will soon observe. The contributors — all sensitive individuals experienced in working with the handicapped — variously speak of *handicapped* children, *disabled* children, *exceptional* children, *vulnerable* children, and children *with special needs*.

There is probably no reason to strive for conformity in the use of any single term. The real point to be made, of course, is that we all need to be aware of our attitudes and the consequences they sometimes cause, thereby minimizing the likelihood that terms like *handicapped* and *disabled* will ever suggest persons of lesser value. Handicapped people, by definition, are limited in the degree to which they can change themselves to meet society's expectations. It is our responsibility—and a measure of our humanity — to make the changes that are needed to create a society we can all share in.

Chapel Hill, N.C.   James L. Paul
Summer 1982

Contributors

John R. Ball, Ed.D., is Professor of Social Work and Criminal Justice, and chairs the Department of Social Work and Correctional Services at East Carolina University in Greenville, N.C. He was Chief Social Worker for the North Carolina Department of Mental Health in Raleigh, Director of the Wright School in Durham, and a social worker for the Baptist Children's Home in Kinston, N.C. He also served as pastor of Peace's Chapel Baptist Church and Corinth Baptist Church in Granville County, N.C.

William M. Cruickshank, Ph.D., is Professor of Child and Family Health, Psychology, and Education at the School of Public Health, University of Michigan. He has published widely in many fields of special education and is a co-author of *Learning Disabilities: The Struggle from Adolescence toward Adulthood.* He is founder and President of the International Academy for Research in Learning Disabilities.

Grace P. Lane, Ph.D., is currently Assistant Professor at Hardin-Simmons University, Abilene, Texas. She has worked with Sunday school classes and church groups from kindergarten to junior high school.

Bobbie B. Lubker, Ph.D., is a member of the faculty, Division of Special Education, the University of North Carolina at Chapel Hill. Her professional interests include the epidemiology of developmental disabilities and populations served by both public health and public education.

James L. Paul, Ed.D., is Professor of Education, Acting Dean of the School of Education, and was chairman of the Division of Special Education of the University of North Carolina, Chapel Hill. Dr. Paul, who also holds a master's degree from Scarritt College, Nashville, has taught and written in the areas of emotional disturbance, autism, learning disabilities, deinstitutionalization, and advocacy.

Patricia B. Porter, Ph.D., is Chief of the Communicative Disorders Section of the University of North Carolina Medical Center's Division for Disorders of Development and Learning, and she is Assistant Professor in the Department of Medical Allied Health Professions. Dr. Porter is actively engaged in the evaluation and training of children.

Ann P. Turnbull, Ph.D., is Acting Associate Director of the Bureau of Child Research and Associate Professor in the Department of Special Education at the University of Kansas. She has published extensively in the field of special education. Her interest in community services has been enhanced by her own experiences as the parent of a mentally retarded child.

The Exceptional Child

1
Growing with a Handicapped Child in the Family and Community
A Parent's Perspective

Ann P. Turnbull

THIS CHAPTER WILL ATTEMPT to introduce the reader to the needs of handicapped children and their families and to suggest helpful responses to those needs from a parent's perspective. It represents a "slice" of the Turnbull family at this point in time.

Needs are dynamic. Change, maturation, learning, and new challenges constantly occur. Although some of our family's needs are chronic and will always be with us in one form or another, others will come and go. Also, our current difficulty in coping with particular needs is no indication that the difficulty always will be present. Growth is a gift. It is the result of experience, time, learning from mistakes, and suffering.

The second purpose of this chapter is to suggest how a "caring community" can respond to the needs of handicapped children and their families. Most efforts to meet the needs associated with handicapped children are relegated to health, education, and social service agencies. Families, neighbors, religious and community organizations, however, represent a support system that is available to most of us — support in the "least restrictive environment" of our daily lives.

The responses are all fairly basic—nothing expensive, or requiring sophisticated technology or advanced training. The responses have a stronger relationship to values than to anything else. Generally, they are based on the premises of decency, respect for differences, and being human and humane. These values represent the best natural resource available to families with handicapped children.

1

FAMILY NEEDS

Jay's Needs

Jay is fourteen years old and has moderate-to-severe mental retardation. In most areas, his developmental skills are those of children aged three to six. Although Jay is my stepson, there is no distinction between my love for him and for my two natural children. He was in a residential institution for three years and has been at home with us on a full-time basis, since Rud and I married seven years ago. Jay's needs now, as an adolescent, are very different from his needs seven years ago, when he was an adorable little boy whom everyone patted on the head and said, "Isn't he cute!"

One of Jay's primary needs now is to be allowed the freedom and opportunity to be himself and to march to the beat of his own drummer. Jay tends to be very passive, quiet, lethargic, even withdrawn at times. Often he likes to live in his own world and does not want to enter our world by participating in activities that the rest of us enjoy. When Jay is by himself, he is convinced that he is in good company. He is happy being alone. In fact, I have often thought that if we wanted to reward Jay for good behavior, we would give him time out in his room. (It is ironic that time out is the punishment that is most effective with his sisters.) Frequently, he likes to sit and watch the world go by. He likes to listen to music, do his own thing, and have the freedom to be himself.

Particularly since Rud and I work very hard during the week, we feel it is very important to devote a large portion of the weekend to family fun. When we gather at the breakfast table each Saturday morning, we plan all sorts of interesting activities for the family. One Saturday morning we presented several options to the children: going to the museum, having a picnic in the park, or going to visit some special friends. And we said, "Jay, what would you like to do?" He sat back in his chair, thought for a minute and said, "Ah, I think I'll sit on my tail and do nothing." I was puzzled by the issue of whether Jay should have the right to do nothing, or whether he needed to be learning, socializing, interacting, doing the things that we think are fun.

There is an inherent conflict between involving Jay in "normalizing" activities and respecting his individual preferences, allowing him sometimes to sit back and watch the world go by. As a parent, I am very much caught in a dilemma between the degree we should enter Jay's world or require him or teach him to enter ours. As I have grown with Jay over the last seven years, I think I have increasingly accepted or respected his preference to be himself and to do what he likes. It is important for us as parents to draw the line between Jay's individual preferences and our hopes for what we wish that he might want to do, between accepting Jay as he is and hoping he were otherwise.

A second of Jay's needs is for security, routine, and familiarity. It is very important to him that meals are always served at the same time, that the closet door is just so ajar, that the curtains are hanging in the same position every day, that the furniture is always in the same place, that the daily activities are predictable. The rest of our family needs variety and adventure. A couple of years ago we decided that it would be fun for the family to go spend a week at the ocean. We decided to rent a cottage and spend our time playing in the waves, collecting shells, and building sand castles. We rented a beach house for quite a substantial fee. At that time, Amy was about three, Kate was an infant, and Jay was twelve. As soon as we arrived, Amy dashed down to the water. When we looked up, she was about the third wave out in the ocean, squealing with delight, oblivious to the fact that she could not swim. We were carrying Kate, and Jay was in the beach house saying, "I want to go home. I want to sleep in my bed in Chapel Hill. No swimming, no ocean, take me home." All week long he was eager to return home. The coercion and unpleasantness of getting Jay to the water was not worth the effort. Meanwhile we kept questioning why we called this a vacation and were even paying for this type of stress. It was an inherent conflict between Jay's need for routine and the family's need for variety.

Jay has another need which all people have—a need for acceptance and for love. I do not think that Jay knows that he is different. If he does, he has not indicated that to us. I wish so much that Jay could communicate some of the things he is feeling. Although he can speak, his language tends to be routinized and concrete. His communication is largely focused on his daily activities and rarely on his feelings, so I do not really know how Jay feels. When we ask him questions about how he feels about something, the standard answer is, "I don't know." Thus, Jay has never indicated that he knows he is different. Sometimes I think that one positive thing about more severe levels of retardation is that children are not as aware of being stared at and not being accepted. Jay has never responded to such episodes as if he were aware of them. It amazes me how he walks into a room of strangers and absolutely expects to be accepted by everyone, even though so often he has not been.

Several years ago we started going to a church whose members tended to be a bit aloof. We liked the service at the church, the minister, and the music, but the social atmosphere was not as supportive as we would have liked. After each Sunday morning service, there was a "coffee hour," a time when people would cluster in their own tight family units, even though it was supposed to be a time for conversation among the members. There were few exchanges—except in Jay's case. The first time we were in church, we had the uncomfortable feeling of not being sure how Jay was going to fit in and not knowing if he was going to be accepted. This was especially true during the coffee hour when, all of a sudden, we heard Jay introducing himself to someone. We saw Jay shaking hands with a very dignified older gentleman and saying, "Hello, this is my son, Jay Turnbull." (That is how he hears us introduce him.) The dignified gentleman was, to say the least, caught off guard, and was mumbling and withdrawing a few steps. Rud turned around and intervened, "Oh, this is my son, Jay, and he has never met a stranger." Whereupon the dignified gentleman said, "Oh, isn't that marvelous?" And rather quickly he disappeared.

Jay does have a positive expectation to be accepted. He loves to shake hands with whomever he meets, and he expects everyone to like him. I think that is a very likeable characteristic. Even though Jay has given us very few clues to suggest that he feels rejected, there is certainly something that lights up in him when he is around people who he knows accept him and love him. And that is one response that has definitely let us know that Jay does feel acceptance.

Last fall, only a few months after we had moved to a new town and new jobs, Rud was in the hospital for two major surgeries. He was there for a month, and I observed that, during that time, our girls could get diverted into activities planned by our neighbors and friends; but Jay had one thing, and one thing alone, on his mind—his dad was not at home. In fact, the first time I took Jay to the hospital to see Rud, Jay sat down in the chair and said, "I am staying here until Daddy comes home." Greater than Jay's need to be in his familiar surroundings is his need to be with the people he loves. That says a lot about the quality of Jay's love. It is abiding, constant, and unwavering. His need is to have that same quality of love reciprocated from other people.

Our Needs as Parents

Setting Jay's needs aside, we may now consider the needs of his parents—my needs and Rud's needs in trying to be the parents that he deserves. One of our major needs is to be confident that Jay will have

access to the educational system, social services, and community organizations, along with the other opportunities that all children need to
grow and to develop. We need to be able to count on the fact that the
services Jay needs are going to be here today and next week and next
year, when he is sixteen years old and when he is fifty-five. At the same
time, we need to learn to live with the fact that we will *never* be able to
make those assumptions, and that is a very difficult fact to cope with.

When Jay first came home at the age of seven, the local public
school did not have a program for mentally retarded children of Jay's age
and level of severity. We were told by an administrator of the school
system that they would try to accommodate him if Rud and I would help
them get funds from the state education agency, locate eight other
children in the area who could enroll in the program, and give them
some leads on where they could find a qualified teacher. The school
system agreed to renovate a large storage area in the administration
building to house the class. We did what was required (which took many
hours of our time), and the class was started.

During the period 1973–1980, a great deal of interest was stirred
on the national level regarding the protection of rights for handicapped
persons. Many lawsuits were brought by parents against states which
excluded handicapped children from public schools. In November of
1975, Congress passed Public Law 94-142, the Education for All
Handicapped Children Act. This legislation, implemented in 1977,
requires that all handicapped children receive a free, appropriate public
education. Essentially, the premise of P.L. 94-142 is that persons who
are less able are not less worthy (Turnbull and Turnbull 1978), and
that they should be provided an opportunity to develop to their fullest
potential.

After P.L. 94-142 was enacted, Rud and I, along with other parents, were able to make the assumption that the schools would serve our
son. We have had four wonderful years of knowing that the public
school would serve Jay, something we take for granted for our two
nonhandicapped daughters.

With the federal government's current de-emphasis of educational and social programs, in favor of greater spending on defense, it is
entirely possible that P.L. 94-142 will be repealed. The gains that were
made and the assumptions that we were able to make for a couple of
years may not be with us for very much longer.

Recently, while at a meeting in Washington, I heard a representative of the Reagan Administration telling a group of educators about
current plans for cutbacks at the federal level. He was saying that P.L.

94-142 probably would be repealed. He told us not to worry, however, because "the thrust is trust"—trust of people at the local and state levels. I felt a knot in my stomach and tears well up in my eyes. I just cannot automatically begin to trust a system whose history is one of the neglect of handicapped persons. As parents and professionals, Rud and I, along with many other parents and professionals, worked very hard in lobbying for P.L. 94-142. We have witnessed firsthand what a quality education has meant for Jay. Now there is a threat that P.L. 94-142 will slip away, and state and local school systems will once again have the option of excluding handicapped children from appropriate education programs. Before P.L. 94-142, Congress found that over one million handicapped children were excluded from school by local and state education agencies. Will it be any different now? Are we returning to a system which only five years ago was found inadequate and discriminating?

Another cliché in the same speech was that even if P.L. 94-142 were repealed, there would still be an accountability system, because "parents can be the watchdog of the system." The watchdog of the system? What a burden! In observing parents of handicapped children who have acted as watchdogs of the system for many years, I have seen the long-term effects on their personalities. It is not something that I want in my life. They become negative. They become adversarial. They become argumentative, and they fight even when there isn't an issue to fight about. Having to be watchdogs totally consumes their personalities. I refuse to let that happen to me. This representative of the administration was suggesting that, while parents of nonhandicapped children go to ballgames, band concerts, and science fairs, parents of handicapped children should go to school board meetings instead. I find it demeaning, fatiguing, frustrating, and inherently unjust constantly to be a watchdog for the public schools in order to insure that they treat my son as they should—as a citizen of the United States.

The second need that we have as parents is for the flexibility, resiliency, and tolerance to live with the fact that our child is different and will always be different. As I think about this need of ours, I realize that I will always be sorrowful when I think about how things might have been for Jay. This does not mean that I do not accept Jay and the fact that he is different. I do accept him in terms of who he is, and I love him very much. But that does not mean that I still do not wish that things had been different for him. Instead of his being in the intermediate class for trainable mentally retarded children, I wonder what it might be like if he were in the eighth grade now, and doing things that other eighth graders do. I have found that my coping strategy is not to let myself think about that. I do not dwell on it, and I keep some emotional distance between that feeling and what I do every day. When I do think about it, though, I have a feeling of sorrow. Our need as parents is to deal constructively with that chronic sorrow.

A third need we have as parents is to feel adequate, to feel that we are good parents. I have never dealt with the initial guilt of bearing a handicapped child, because Jay is my stepson. I was able to skip that stage which, as many parents have reported, is quite devastating. But there is another type of guilt which I have experienced, and that is the guilt that sometimes comes from asking the questions:

Have I done enough to help Jay?

Have I taken him to enough doctors?

Have I gotten him enough therapy?

Have I spent enough hours interacting and stimulating him?

Have I spent enough time planning and following through on his IEP (individualized education program)?

Have I gone to enough Association for Retarded Citizens meetings?

Let's face it. I think that society, in general, expects parents of handicapped children to be super-parents, and I think that we also expect it of ourselves. Sometimes parents set themselves up for thinking they can assume all the responsibilities that are required at home, plus all the program development and advocacy required in the community, plus all of the personal coping in dealing with the child's handicap, and still come across as the "well-adjusted, coping parent." Sometimes I feel that it is a lot to handle. I have learned that being able to express frustration and anger is essential. Also, setting realistic expectations is incredibly important in regard to coping and adjusting to the problems that are posed by a handicapping condition.

Needs of Siblings

Our nonhandicapped girls, Amy and Kate, are six and three. Amy is beginning to be curious about Jay's difference, and I expect Kate soon to experience the same type of curiosity. I think one of their first needs, as this awareness is evolving, is to understand what a handicap is, at their level of comprehension. At the same time they need to learn respect for difference (not just tolerance for it), respect for the fact that Jay needs to be himself and to exercise his own preferences.

The insights of Amy, our six-year-old, have both amazed and inspired me. Two years ago she was in a parent cooperative preschool in which parents would work in the classroom for one morning every week and a half. On our preschool mornings, Rud and I would often teach a lesson about handicapping conditions. The children learned some songs and learned to sign their names. We took a friend who was in a wheelchair, and he played wheelchair basketball with the children. A blind friend also instructed the children in braille and showed them his braille books. Amy and her friends had all sorts of experiences, and we found it was a wonderful age to introduce these sorts of human differences. We did that because we wanted Amy to *learn* about handicaps, not just at home, but also in the "real world" of her peer group. We did not talk about mental retardation at preschool because it is so abstract. It was much easier to talk with four-year-olds about wheelchairs than about a brain that works slowly. We had decided not to talk to Amy about Jay's problems until she asked. We felt that her questions would be an indication that she was really ready to explore this issue. She never asked because it was all very normal to her. That was the only way Jay had ever been. Her friends started asking her, "Why does your brother act so strange?" "Why can't he talk clearly?" "Why does he dangle his fingers in front of his face?" Since Amy did not know how to answer these questions, we decided that it was time to plunge in and to talk with her about Jay's mental retardation.

One evening Amy and I were chatting and I said, "Amy, there's another handicap that we haven't talked about, and it is one that I think is important for you to know about. It's mental retardation. Mental retardation means that someone's brain is damaged in some way so that they learn more slowly than other people." Very nonchalantly she said, "I don't know anyone like that." And I said, "Yes, you do. Jay is mentally retarded." She was shocked and disbelieving. I asked her if she had ever wondered why she was able to do things at five that Jay could not do at thirteen. Well, no, she had never wondered that. I asked her if she could think of some of those things, and she rather quickly listed them. We talked about the fact that Jay has not yet learned to do these things because his brain is damaged and works slowly. I told her that he could always make progress, but that he would always learn more slowly than most other children. Amy asked how her brain and her little sister's brain worked. I told her their brains worked fast. She thought for a while and she said, "Mommy, is it like my record player?" I said, "What do you mean?" She responded, "There is that button on the side and if you push it one way the record goes slowly, and if you push it another way the record goes fast." And I said, "Amy, I've never thought about that, but that's a wonderful example. Brains work on different speeds just like record players. Sometimes they work slowly and sometimes they work fast." She thought for a minute, and then she said that I was failing to tell her one very important thing: "It plays music on both speeds. Jay might be slow and Kate and I might be fast; but, Mommy, all three of us still play music." I could have thought for twenty-five years and never come up with that kind of example.

This does not mean that in the future Amy is not going to be frustrated or even embarrassed at times with Jay, but I think it is an indication she is learning something very important about living with imperfection. Often, as parents, I think we rob our children of experiences in living with imperfection by taking it away, by making everything nice and beautiful and proper so that they do not learn to deal with differences or deviations. Once they grow up, however, they are going to have to deal with the imperfections in their own lives and in society. I have heard other parents of handicapped children say that, as their nonhandicapped children grew up, they really felt that they were more able to have the flexibility and resiliency to respect differences because of their early experiences. I think I really see that developing with Amy and Kate, and it makes me feel very good. Undoubtedly, they still have a tremendous need to understand and explore the implications of Jay's handicap in far greater detail.

It concerned me for a while, after that initial conversation, that months passed by and Amy did not mention anything about Jay's handicap again. Finally one evening she was upset about something else and was crying. As we were talking, she stated that something else was wrong, but she could not tell me about it because it would make me sad. I reiterated to her that all of her feelings are accepted and supported, and I encouraged her to share them with me. She burst out crying and said, "I wish Jay was not my brother. What I really mean, Mommy, is that I wish he were not mentally retarded. Don't you wish it, too?" She was beginning to deal with some of the grief that things were not "right." I think she is beginning to work through these feelings, but I realize that adjusting to Jay's difference will be a continuing need of both our girls.

In regard to sibling needs, Amy and Kate also need support and acceptance from their peers and neighbors. When other children are playing at our house and ask questions about Jay, our girls will need to be able to answer those questions. "Why does your brother act so strange?" When that question is asked now, they can say his brain works slowly and that's why he does not talk as well as other people, but there are other things which he can do well.

Needs of Extended Family

Our extended family, particularly Jay's grandparents, have a tremendous need for access to knowledge about mental retardation, about Jay's prognosis, and expectations for his future. They are very curious about what Jay will be able to do when he is an adult, and they also want to know how much academic content he will be able to master in school. Sometimes it is hard for them to live with the ambiguity of our answers to those questions and the fact that we really do not know what the future holds. When Rud and I were children, our parents were able to assume that we would attain academic success in high school, go to college, prepare for careers, leave home, and assume responsibility for jobs and family. Now, we are asking them to learn to be grandparents to a grandchild they did not expect to have, a grandchild for whom they can have none of those hopes and expectations. They must have adaptability in learning to alter the assumptions they made in raising their children in regard to future planning for their grandson. And, like us, they have a need to learn to live with a future that cannot be entirely planned, due to the possibility of changes in federal legislation; services which we have for Jay today may be gone tomorrow.

Additionally, I have found that Jay's grandparents and relatives have a need for support from their friends, as they go through many of the same adjustment problems that we do in terms of grief, resentment, and frustration. Sometimes we are not the best people to help them with those feelings, because we are using our psychic and emotional energy to cope with our own adjustment. Again, it can come down to an issue of priority. Who is in greatest need for support? Sometimes they are strong and are able to support us; at other times, the relationship is reversed. In addition to our support as they go through the process of acceptance of Jay, they need other people who are sensitive to their concerns about Jay.

The extended family also needs to know about the impact of Jay on our immediate family. Currently, Jay is having some rather violent seizures, where he is injurious to himself and sometimes to his sisters. The seizures are rare; however, they are a big problem when they do occur. If we do not share our worry and concern with our family after the occurrence of the seizures, we cut off communication and deny them an opportunity to share our feelings. Yet if we do tell them, it is quite a burden for them to worry about the safety of Jay and the girls, as well as the impact of this stress on Rud and me. I think it is particularly hard for the extended family in our mobile society, when distance is great and they cannot come to visit and see that things are okay. They have to rely on phone calls and letters from us, which is another reason why support from their immediate caring community is important.

RESPONDING TO NEEDS

Responses within the Family

Responding to personal needs must start within the family. I think we need to reach out for other people, such as neighbors, friends, professionals, and people in religious and community organizations; but there has to be a core at home who can help meet these needs. One thing that is so important is to be able to share with each other, knowing that it is okay to be sad, frustrated, and angry. When we share those feelings, it must be in an open and honest way. At the same time, it must be recognized that wallowing in negative feelings is futile and unproductive. It is essential to share feelings, but then to move expediently into analyzing them and figuring out how to resolve them. Figuring out alternatives for solving problems prevents us from going down in quicksand in regard to emotional dilemmas. At the same time, it is just as important for us to share the joys and progress and to accentuate the positive in regard to Jay's development.

I also think that it is appropriate not to fall into the trap of being a "retarded" family, with the whole family engrossed in being a "watchdog for the system," reading test reports, dealing with deviations in development, and all the other things associated with retardation. An appropriate response is to develop other interests and outlets, to have time away from handicapped children, and to have a larger world than simply the world of retardation.

Another thing that is so necessary is for there to be "unconditional love" within the family. Erich Fromm, in *The Art of Loving,* describes unconditional love as not having to be earned or even deserved, but as a non-negotiable fact of life which will be ever-present. Another type of love which Fromm describes is "motherly love"; however, I think it can also be characterized as "family love." I really like the example he gives in comparing this love to the concept of the "promised land," which has been described as "flowing with milk and honey." As Fromm points out, "milk" is one type of love which is the symbol of care and affirmation.

Certainly, that is so necessary to have in the family, but is it really enough? He also talks about "honey" symbolizing the sweetness of life, the love for it and the happiness of being alive. I think if families can generate both "milk and honey," the core of support they can provide to each other will be incredibly important.

Responses from Neighbors

I really value neighbors and believe that a tremendous support system is available from the persons who live in close proximity to us. Neighborhoods are more than a lot of houses or apartments which are close to each other. Rather, they can truly provide a network of a caring community.

Although we have lived in our present neighborhood for only nine months, we have derived a tremendous sense of support from it. Prior to our move, I had never thought about what it would be like to move to a new community and neighborhood and introduce Jay to total strangers. It really pointed out to me the need for neighbors with knowledge and familiarity with handicapping conditions.

I think neighbors can help parents and handicapped children by reaching out to them and providing unsolicited support. One of our neighbors in particular has done an incredible job of reaching out to Jay. Last fall when Rud was in the hospital, Steve called and invited Jay for pizza and ice cream. He said that he knew Jay must be missing his Dad, and perhaps he would enjoy going out with just "the guys" so the two of them would really have a chance to get to know each other. Steve will never know how much that meant. When I told Rud about it, he cried. I cried about it, too — wonderful, happy tears because someone was seeking Jay out. Rarely is Jay sought out for himself and not as part of the family unit.

Another example of reaching out occurred when Steve and his family came over to our house for an Easter egg hunt. As soon as they arrived, Steve shook Jay's hand, gave the camera to his wife, and said, "I want you to take my picture with Jay. I want a picture of just the two of us." Why was this so special? Rarely had anyone wanted their picture taken with Jay before. Jay broke out in a big grin and *knew*—really knew —that Steve is his friend. It meant so much to Jay, and it meant so much to us that Steve was seeking Jay out in that way. A special ingredient of Steve's relationship with Jay is that it is built on an awareness of Jay's individuality and a respect for him. Steve does not feel sorry for Jay; rather, he *likes* Jay. And that makes all the difference.

During this period of cutbacks in services for handicapped people, another supportive response from neighbors is helping to advocate for the child. For example, neighbors could help parents be a "watchdog of the system" by supporting special education programs in the local schools. We once had a neighbor who wrote a letter to our congressman when there was a threat of a cutback in federal money. She stated in her letter, "I have a neighbor, Jay Turnbull, whose educational program is supported by these funds. His progress has been remarkable. Please provide him an opportunity to continue to grow and develop..." She sent us a copy of the letter. It really made me aware of her support of Jay and of us as his parents. I appreciated it tremendously, and I am sure if Jay were at a level so that he could understand, he would have appreciated it as much as we did.

It is very important in the neighborhood and with friends to be able to share concerns openly. I remember being at a dinner party a year or so ago with two friends who had teenage children. They were lamenting the fact that their teenagers had to stay at band practice late in the afternoon, spent so much time in the bathroom blowing their hair dry, and played their stereo too loudly. I know that adolescence is hard, and I know that when our two girls are teenagers, I will probably lament those same things; but as I sat there listening to them, I felt very isolated and alone. I was thinking that I would give anything for those sorts of problems. I was worrying about Jay's seizures, which started at puberty, whether the vacation would be too stressful for him, and about the fact that he still could not write his last name. Their concerns seemed so trivial to me. In situations like that, I typically do not say much. I have learned that most people do not want to hear my concerns, because it makes them feel uncomfortable. The most typical responses that I have had when sharing my gut-level concerns about Jay with neighbors or friends are for them to try to cut the conversation off, or to make a nervous, humorous remark and change the subject. Another typical response is to relate the concern or problem to their nonhandicapped child and say the problem applies to all children, not just handicapped children. Friends and neighbors sometimes want to make things okay by simply saying that the behavior is not really different, when the truth of the matter is that it *is* different.

When friends share experiences with parents of handicapped children, one of the most important things for them to do is to *listen*. In cases of deviant behavior, they don't have to try to make the behavior okay; they cannot make it okay. When parents share, they are not usually looking for an answer; they are looking for support for their feelings and for the fact that something was a very hard thing to experience. It is important to listen, acknowledge concerns, and offer support and advice if appropriate. I wish more of my friends were able to share that part of my world with me.

Responses from Religious Organizations

Religious organizations—churches and synagogues—can provide a wonderful instructional and socializing milieu for handicapped children and their families. Of all organizations in the community, they should be open and receptive to meeting humans needs. An obvious response is to structure religious education programs so they can accommodate chidren with various handicaps. Such accommodation involves architectural access, as well as modifying programs to meet the special needs of handicapped children. Other chapters in this book address these issues in more detail. My suggestions will focus on how I, as a parent, would like the churches we come in contact with to respond to Jay's needs, as well as the needs of our family members.

First, I should mention that Jay loves to put on his blazer and tie and go to church. It is truly one of the highlights of his week. He is extremely well behaved in church—much more so than many children of his age. He enjoys the music and frequently hums or chants (since he cannot read the words from the hymnal). Another highlight of church for Jay is being able to shake hands with people before and after the service. One of my favorite things to do with Jay is to attend church with him.

In our experiences of participating actively in several different churches, Rud and I have not yet found a church that had a systematic plan for including handicapped children in the church school program. Whereas we could always make the assumption that there would be a program for Kate and Amy, we could not make the same assumption for Jay. It has not been that our churches have tried to exclude Jay; however, they have not responded with appropriate alternatives for him. Thus, it has been our responsibility to find out about the church school program, make suggestions on where and how Jay might participate, and sometimes train the teachers to accommodate him. The problem with this is that once again we cannot make assumptions, and our energy and frustration tolerance is limited in terms of how many programs we can initiate: public school, after-school care while we work, group homes, community recreation, political action, and the countless other responsibilities which parents of handicapped children must assume. We have learned that we have to set priorities, realizing that we cannot work on everything at once. At some periods when we have started going to a new church, we have found that it took time before we could muster the energy to start negotiating a "new system." Thus, our alternative was to have Jay attend church with us, but not to participate in the church school program. I longed to have the church school director approach Jay and invite him into a program or explain options to me on how he could be included. This, however, has never happened.

One strategy for religious organizations in responding to this need is to develop a plan for incorporating handicapped children into their program. Rather than waiting until a handicapped person joins their congregation and then wondering where to "put" them, a committee of church members knowledgeable in special education could systematically develop alternatives and also conduct training of the religious education teachers to enhance the success of the alternatives. Such a committee would serve to relieve parents of this responsibility. And for most parents, being able to assume that the church would serve their child without their having to work out all the arrangements and details would be like receiving a cherished gift.

Accommodating the handicapped child in a religious program is necessary, but it is not sufficient. As I mentioned earlier, handicapped children have a tremendous need for acceptance and respect. Jay had a wonderful church school experience when he was twelve and thirteen years old. He was "mainstreamed" into a fifth grade class taught by Grace Lane, the author of one of the other chapters in this book. Grace was able to adapt the instructional aspects of the program so that Jay could benefit from them; but, even more importantly, Jay knew that she liked him and welcomed him as a full-fledged member of the class. He always looked forward to going, and it was as much to hear her cheery "Good Morning" and see the twinkle in her eyes as it was to be part of the lesson. Grace lifted his spirits and helped him feel good about himself. What could be a more constructive outcome of a religious education program?

Grace is an extremely skilled special educator. It gave me so much confidence as a parent to know that she felt comfortable with Jay. Most teachers, however, will need training in adapting their curriculum to the needs of handicapped children. In fact, the purpose of this book is to address that training need.

In addition to the teacher's need for training, other church members may welcome information on the nature of handicapping conditions and on ways they can positively interact with handicapped persons. From our experience, we have found that most people are extremely sensitive to Jay after they have had an opportunity to learn about his needs and get to know him. It is not unusual for people to be a bit afraid of situations with which they are unfamiliar. I believe that a major strategy for enhancing the acceptance of handicapped persons is to increase people's knowledge about their needs. The religious education program provides a golden opportunity for such consciousness-raising: instruction can be provided in the classes of both children and adults. Handicapped adults can be valuable instructional resources; religious education leaders could seek them out and invite them to share their experiences and talk about the positive and negative aspects of relationships between handicapped and nonhandicapped persons.

One sure way to enhance the members' familiarity with handicapped persons is to include them in religious programs. Because of the severity of their handicaps, some persons may need to be in a specialized religious education program similar to special education classes in the public schools. Such a program would be attended only by handicapped persons. My preference for Jay, however, is to have him integrated or mainstreamed into a class with nonhandicapped children. I think such an arrangement has benefits for both Jay and his peers. For Jay, it provides an opportunity to have friends who are not handicapped. He can be stimulated by them in terms of their language and concept development. Jay's peers, on the other hand, can learn from him about differences, about the gift of their own health, and about Jay's ability to cope and survive despite his limitations. Also, from Jay, they can learn to share his excitement in going to church, and they will have a model of almost perfect church behavior!

Responses from Community Organizations

I believe that involvement in community organizations, particularly community recreational programs, is tremendously important in meeting the needs of handicapped children and their families. For handicapped children, they provide an opportunity to develop hobbies, leisure time interests, talents, and social skills in learning to interact with peers. For the parents of handicapped children, community recreation provides assistance and support in meeting the recreation and leisure time needs of their children. It can also provide them with respite care, or a break from the fulltime responsibility of caring for their child.

My suggestions for how community recreational programs can respond to the needs of handicapped children and their families are similar to those included in the previous section on religious programs: accommodating handicapped children by providing architectural access and program modification; making provisions for including handicapped children; rather than depending upon parents to initiate the alternatives for inclusion; insuring that handicapped children are accepted and respected; training teachers; making provisions to mainstream handicapped children when possible; and fostering the development of positive attitudes on the part of nonhandicapped children toward their handicapped peers.

In thinking back over Jay's involvement in community recreation programs, one experience which stands out is a six-week summer day camp program which he attended several years ago. It was sponsored by the city recreation department and was primarily developed for nonhandicapped children. We talked with the recreation coordinator about enrolling Jay, and she agreed "to give it a try." She told us that the counselors did not have special training related to handicapping conditions, and that she was making no promises that it would work out. On the first day of camp, Rud and I were nervous about whether Jay would fit in, but Jay was not nervous in the least—simply excited. When we took him, we stayed to talk with the counselors. We explained to them about the fact that Jay was mentally retarded and had some special needs. They were mostly high school and college students, and they were a bit harried by the confusion of the first day of camp. They assured us that they would give it their best and that time would tell whether Jay could handle it. Immediately we noticed some of the other children staring at Jay and trying to figure him out. When we left, Jay was sitting in the middle of the floor by himself. On our way to the car, I remember questioning why we were putting Jay and ourselves through this. We wanted to protect him from being rejected, and it was stressful for us as parents to "give it a try."

The day dragged by very slowly as we kept wondering what was happening. When we arrived to pick Jay up, Raymond, one of the counselors, started walking out to the car. Rud and I said to each other, "Get ready for the news. Here it comes. They are not going to let Jay come back." Raymond leaned in the window of the car and enthusiastically stated, "Jay is a great camper! You know, you said he was mentally retarded, but I don't believe it. Today we went on a hike. The hike was long, and we were hot. Jay might have been last in line, but he's no quitter. When we got back, I shook his hand and congratulated him. I tell you one thing — there's nothing retarded about that boy's smile!" That not only sounded like music to our ears, it was a full-blown symphony! It conveyed to us that they accepted and respected Jay for who he was. That was the first day of one of the best summers Jay ever had. Raymond became the center of Jay's life for six weeks, and on the last day of camp all of us shed some tears when we parted. However, it did not end there, because the confidence Raymond gave Jay has helped him in countless other situations. And, as Raymond said, "Jay's taught me more this summer than I have taught him."

I think it is worth pointing out that we enrolled Jay in the same program the following summer and it did not work out. There were more children, fewer counselors, and no Raymond. We tried it for three or four days, and it was obvious to everyone that it simply was not going to work. As an alternative, Jay participated in a recreational program designed solely for handicapped children. At that point in time, the specialized program met his needs far better than the mainstreamed one.

As a parent, I recognize the tremendous need for options and choices. In situations and programs in which Jay can successfully be mainstreamed or integrated with nonhandicapped children, I generally prefer such a placement. His needs, however, frequently require a program specially designed for handicapped children. I want Jay to be able to move back and forth between mainstreamed and specialized "worlds." Each has its unique benefits and drawbacks, and I feel that taking advantage of both options is important.

In summary, this chapter has been a parent's perspective on needs in a caring community and responses to those needs. It should be reiterated that the needs reported here are our needs at the present time. Our needs are very different now from what they were when Jay was born, or seven years ago when he first returned home from a residential institution. This would have been a completely different chapter if I had written it seven years ago. During this time, I have learned a great deal from Jay. For me, it has been a period of doubting, of struggling, of learning, of maturing, of questioning, of making mistakes, of trying to resolve again, of questioning again, or growing, and of feeling satisfaction over our gains. And I will have to say that while the process of writing this chapter has been very therapeutic for me, I cried when I wrote it. There were tears of joy in looking back over our experiences and, as with anything else, there were also tears of sorrow. I think our needs are real, but through them I have gotten to know myself and my family in ways that I never, otherwise, would have done. Furthermore, just as needs are ever present, so are responses to those needs. Responses come in many packages—some, thankfully, tied with red bows. Such responses from the family, neighbors and friends, and religious and community organizations are tremendously supportive in helping handicapped persons and their families cope with some of their special needs.

Overall, the coping strategy which I have found to be the most helpful is based on something which my mother shared with me when I graduated from high school. It is as follows: "Happiness is my wish for you, but my wishes cannot give it. Nor can it come from outward circumstances. Happiness can come only from yourself, from the spirit that is within you. You cannot choose what changes and chances are to befall you in the coming years, but you can choose the spirit in which you will meet them."

In my opinion, the single most important coping strategy in growing with a handicapped child is the ability to choose one's attitude in responding to a given set of circumstances—to determine whether to give in to the circumstances or to stand up to them, and, after that decision is made, to determine your attitude about them. It is through this self-determination, which is bolstered tremendously by the support of family, neighbors and friends, along with religious and community organizations, that handicapped persons and their families have the greatest potential for success.

REFERENCE

Turnbull, H. R., and Turnbull, A. P. *Free Appropriate Public Education: Law and Implementation.* Denver: Love, 1978.

2
Exceptional Children
Who Are They?

William M. Cruickshank

EXCEPTIONAL CHILDREN have been with us since prehistoric times; their presence in our societies is not a new occurrence. In our age, however, we have become more aware of these citizens as social attitudes have become more understanding of them. Society's responsibility to the handicapped is now something which is accepted by many, many persons. Witness the myriad of campaigns on behalf of the disabled—the lavish TV and radio fund appeals, and the projects of such voluntary groups as the Lions Club (on behalf of the blind), the Rotary Club (the crippled child), the Civitan Club (mental retardation), and many other private and professional organizations. This was not always the case.

There were times, for example, when churches turned their backs on those with severe physical and mental differences. "God created man in His own image," the Bible tells us. Men and women who were physically handicapped, emotionally ill, mentally retarded, or who in other ways deviated from the Christian concept of God's perfection were often considered outside the province of religion. During the Puritan era in the United States, the existing organized religions routinely held the handicapped person in disregard. Emotionally disturbed women were persecuted as witches in colonial times. The early reports by commissioners of county poor houses and county jails in the eighteenth and nineteenth centuries are full of recommendations to separate the handicapped residents from the others. "A person with fits is staked out in the rear of the building," stated a Massachusetts county jail commissioner in 1821.

Reports similar to this are easy to find. Heroic women and men such as Dorothea Dix, Samuel Gridley Howe, and others fought hard to change these attitudes. In large part, they were successful. Gradually, religious and community groups began to reach out to provide services in ways they knew best at the time. The Catholic Church, particularly the members of some religious orders, provided educational and residential facilities for deaf and mentally retarded children, and later, learning-disabled children and youth. Today there are excellent Lutheran schools for deaf children, and the members of the Shriners organization maintain vast programs for crippled and burned children. Other semireligious-sponsored health and educational programs are supported by individuals (the Andy Williams, Bing Crosby, or Danny Thomas golf tournaments) and by organizations on a local and national basis. This was not always the case. True, some religious groups built homes and institutions for the handicapped, but these were essentially custodial in nature. The educational programs as a primary function of residential facilities came, for the most part, in the latter part of the twentieth century.

By the early 1900s, public schools were beginning to provide some, albeit separate, educational programs in the home community for disabled children. We can obtain some insight into the changing attitudes of society toward the handicapped child by examining the names of some of these institutions which purported to serve them. In Michigan, for example, a facility for delinquent boys was first known as the House of Correction for Juvenile Offenders. One can almost hear whips crack! This oppressive title was imposed on the institution around 1850. Later, it became known as the Boys' Reform School. *Correction* and *reform* were the key words. Subsequently, as society's attitudes began to become more humane, the school was called the Boys Training School; education begins to creep in. Ultimately, the facility was renamed the Michigan Boys' Vocational School, and now education, retraining, and vocational placement are the key concepts (although the title was many years ahead of the actual program). In upstate New York, there is an institution originally known as the Rome School for the Deaf, Dumb, Blind and Idiot. Michigan had a somewhat similarly titled facility; every problem from the neck up was treated within one facility.

That is not the case in the 1980s, although there still are many misconceptions of what handicapped individuals' problems truly are. Let us examine terminology, for example:

What it used to be and still often is:	*What it is and should be:*
1. Deaf and dumb, deaf-mute	1. Deaf, hard of hearing, or hearing impaired *children*
2. Retardates	2. Mentally retarded *children*
3. Feebleminded	3. Educable mentally retarded *children* or *youth*, or *children* with retarded mental development
4. Idiots	4. Profoundly retarded *children*
5. Imbeciles	5. Trainable or severely retarded *children*
6. Morons	6. Educable mentally retarded *children*
7. Fits	7. Seizures
8. Blind	8. Blind, partially sighted, or low vision *children*
9. Learning disabled, brain injured, minimal brain damage (MBD)	9. *Children* with learning disabilities
10. Insane	10. Emotionally disturbed *children*

How would you like to be called a *retardate*? It is hard enough to live with mental retardation; but it is worse to have a negative label placed on oneself or on one's child.

Notice that the terms — not an entirely complete list — in the right-hand column are positive in that they emphasize children or youth. Handicapped or disabled children are first and foremost *children;* hence, we call them retarded children, deaf children, learning-disabled children. Old terms reflect a lack of knowledge and compassion toward disabled persons; new terms contain a significant element of mental health.

For example, the terms *handicapped, disabled,* and *atypical* are better expressed in the term"exceptional child," although the latter in the minds of many persons is only used with the gifted child. However, increasing numbers of universities and textbooks utilize the word *exceptional* to designate the total population of those with varying types of physical and mental differences. The goal is to find and utilize words which carry implications of good mental health.

We have said these children have the basic characteristics and individual differences of all children. Some are tall, others short. Some are blond, others brunet. Some are thin, others overweight. Some are "straight," others "gay" or homosexual. The patterns, or any dimension, appear to reflect the population as a whole. No matter what their disability, they are young people with needs identical to their normal friends. As a group, recognizing normal individual differences in growth patterns, they reach puberty and adolescence at about the same time as do their normal friends. They have the same needs in the area of human sexuality and fulfillment as do physically normal youth. The handicapped young person is not asexual, as many parents and professional people believe or would like to believe. Their needs for social activities are identical to those of normal children, i.e., for religious education classes and activities, 4-H clubs, Boy and Girl Scout troops, summer camps, and similar youth groups.

While there may be some things that are difficult or impossible for handicapped youth to accomplish within the group, there is absolutely nothing that prevents them from becoming members. For the most part, they will be able to participate quite fully in the activities of the group, and in some cases they may surpass the skills and abilities of so-called normal youths. When differences do exist, the responsibility belongs primarily to the normal individuals to learn to listen, to learn to anticipate, or in other ways learn to facilitate the activities of the exceptional child, youth or adult.

GROUP CHARACTERISTICS

It is not the intention of this section to discuss in detail the characteristics of certain clinical problems. However, because disabled children and youth are making their appearance in community public school classes more and more frequently, it is presumed that they will also be knocking on the doors of religious institutions and youth groups and requesting admission in greater numbers.

While threat is never a good mechanism, it is appropriate to point out that in the activist society which characterizes the United States, class-action suits are not infrequently brought in the courts against institutions such as schools, and in support of traditionally disadvantaged groups such as racial and religious minorities and women. In recent years, there have been court suits in behalf of girls who wished to play baseball on a Little League team, or even football on formerly all-boys teams. Handicapped children and youth (or their parents) are likewise quite willing to file class-action suits to protect their right to a share of society's services and benefits. It is so easy to assimilate these children into formal youth groups, that it is completely unnecessary and unwise to have to experience the cost and embarrassment of a court action, the outcome of which can be guessed in advance most of the time.

Mentally Retarded Children

Mental retardation is traditionally measured along a continuum and is often designated by the intelligence quotient. It is usually believed that a young person with an intelligence quotient of 115 or above will be able to complete college work with about a C average. I.Q.s commonly occur in the range between 120–180, although they are rare at the upper extreme, or genius level. If one considers an I.Q. of about 106 as the national average, quotients below that point drop down into the levels of retardation. Those with quotients ranging from 85–105 are often referred to as slow-learning children, and those with quotients between 60 and 85 as educable retarded children. Children and youth with intelligence levels below 60 are severely retarded or profoundly retarded and probably will not make their appearance in organized youth groups.

There is absolutely no reason why educable or slow-learning children should not be assimilated into organized community groups; although certainly the normal children in these groups, their parents, and perhaps friends may need some orientation to these and other exceptional children. Two excellent sets of films to trigger discussions before the first exceptional child appears in a group are "Like You; Like Me" and "People You'd Like to Know," both available from the Encyclopaedia Britannica Educational Corporation in Chicago, Illinois. Many schools own their own copies and probably would be willing to lend them. These films cover many more topics than mental retardation. The former series is concerned with young children, the latter with youths in the junior and senior high school grades.

To return to mentally retarded youth, these young people are often most helpful to an organized group. They will contribute to their maximum capacity. They make friends and appreciate friendship extended to them. There is nothing contagious about mental retardation.

They may need an extra pat on the back, and leadership must be careful not to ask them to perform skills which are beyond their capability. They work well with a friend who has normal capacities and judgment. If reading and number concepts are required, they may need assistance from an adult or an older group friend.

Mental retardation is often found in combination with all other types of handicapping conditions. When this happens, the individual is called multiply handicapped, for example, a mentally retarded blind youth, or mentally retarded, cerebral-palsied children. If these children make their appearance in social groups, as they do in public school classes, the leadership should obtain counsel from those who are specialists or who have experience in integrating these more severely disabled young people into the group being considered. Even these young people can participate in most social activities, can learn to swim, to tell stories, to help around a campfire, to make their beds, set up camp, and join in other activities of youth groups.

The Crippled Child

Depending upon their level of intelligence, most crippled children can participate in organized youth activities to a great extent. The term "crippled child" covers a tremendous number of different clinical problems, not one of them contagious. Within this mixed classification are a few post-polio (poliomyelitis) children, who, because of religious belief or other reasons, were not vaccinated. Also included are those with cerebral palsy, a neurological condition usually occurring before or at birth; children with muscular dystrophy (often in more advanced states confined to a wheelchair); multiple sclerosis (also progressive); spina bifida (a neurological congenital defect to the spine, and often progressive and accompanied with mental retardation); club foot (no major problem to a youth group or its leader); and a myriad of other clinical problems, both congenital and acquired.

Among teenagers, motorcycle or bicycle accidents, water skiing accidents, and automobile accidents may leave the youth in serious condition, thus requiring even more the support of organized religious and youth activities. There are ways in which even the most seriously disabled can participate in social groups, such as dancing while in wheelchairs, taking tickets at the door, helping to organize the activity initially, and in other ways coming to feel that they are wanted and needed. Sports activities such as swimming, bowling, track events, and even basketball and baseball from wheelchairs are not completely ruled out for even the most seriously disabled youth. They do have girl friends and boy friends; they do marry and have children. They need social experiences with the opposite sex as a basis for their ultimate personal decisions.

When the leader of a youth group is in doubt, he or she should ask! School personnel, parents, social agency representatives, college and university special education and rehabilitation faculty members can all be helpful in assisting the leader of a religious group, nursery school, or a 4-H club, and they are willing to do so.

The Blind Child or Youth

For too many years, the blind children of this nation and others have been cloistered in tightly supervised residential schools, often separated from their parents for months on end. In more recent years, these children have been integrated into regular neighborhood schools and grades, usually to the advantage of everyone. Multiply handicapped children or youth, those whose blindness is associated with severe mental retardation or cerebral palsy, may not have this opportunity as frequently, but blind children with reasonably good intelligence can participate in ways which often bring awe to the faces of accompanying adults. They bowl, swim, play games of jacks and marbles, ski, fly kites, jump rope, wrestle, participate in foot races, erect tents, cook outdoors, raise animals, enter into Junior Achievement programs, and do many other things. How many sighted children can study at night in a pitch black room? Blind youths can, and frequently do. They can attend dances, and do. They can date, and do. They can get into trouble just as sighted children do. They can *not* drive cars or motorcycles, and don't. They can attend church, and sometimes do. They can go on hikes with canes, dogs, or electronic probes, and do. The blind child or youth is not difficult to integrate into normal youth groups or activities. Some have outstanding skills at the piano, organ, or other musical instruments, and can contribute much to the group as a whole.

Blindness has its limitations, of course. Sighted friends and adults need to be alert to situations which could be dangerous or injurious to the child who is not fully oriented to a new camping site, new building, or to unfamiliar stairs, swimming pools, low-hanging branches, and other unexpected hazards. If a blind youth has had a good program of mobility training and orientation, he or she will be able to deal with new environmental situations quite adequately. Most disabled adolescents tell us that it is the adult who impresses upon them the limitations of their disabilities — realistic or imagined — not school-age friends. The latter present challenges; the former, cautions.

Some adults also experience this from well-intended adult friends. An individual who had experienced a series of heart attacks had problems with overzealous friends, who rushed to open doors, to assist him into automobiles, and cautioned him about walking up stairs (never down), who urged him to carry one piece of wood at a time to the living room fireplace, who constantly, in the best spirit, reminded him of restrictions. He ultimately had to be direct and firm with his wife and close associates, whom he perceived as restrictors of his behavior. The good intentions of adults are not always seen as such by the disabled individual who seeks personal independence.

A friend of the writer lost the use of an eye. "Isn't it wonderful," someone told him, "that you can drive an automobile." The individual with the remaining good eye refrained from telling his friend that he was also taking flying lessons, an activity approved by the Civil Aeronautics Board!

The blind child and youth can usually do more rather than less. Those who work with blind or partially sighted youth should observe what the young person can do before any attempt is made to caution him or her against doing things. The blind can eat; can cut their own meat; can dress; can take showers and bathe; can go for walks and hikes; can take care of animals; can play many card games (there are decks of cards with braille imprinted on them); and for the most part can do most of the things which normal children of the same chronological age can do.

Epilepsy or Convulsive Disorders

Children who experience convulsions or epilepsy are found everywhere. There used to be a stigma attached to individuals with epilepsy. But today, with the careful use of medication, most of these children and youth live happy, normal lives, and seizures do not get in their way, and are not normally seen in the community. Epilepsy, per se, is not a valid excuse for excluding these children from normal activities of childhood, nor for stigmatizing them in any way. Society has an obligation to understand the nature of this condition, and to accept these young persons fully and completely.

If a youngster with a history of epilepsy applies, for example, to become a member of a Girl Scout troop, the leader might wish to discuss with her parents what may appear to be important information regarding the problem. How often does she take medication? When? Does she remember to take her own medication, or does she have to be reminded? How often do seizures occur (probably rarely)? Is there a pattern to their occurrence? What is the procedure to be followed if a seizure occurs? Does she have serious seizures (grand mal) or minor seizures (petit mal)? The answers to these questions will be reassuring most of the time and tend toward normal childhood behavior. The information received should put the adult at ease. Sometimes, the leader may wish to assign another youth as a "buddy" to the one with a history of seizures. Most arrangements such as this have been dropped after a period of time, when there appears to be no major problems. Young people with epilepsy go on dates. They ride bicycles. They drive cars. After an individual has been seizure-free for a three-year period, many states have laws that prohibit their being termed epileptic. The individual with epilepsy is more normal than abnormal and should be considered from that point of view.

We have mentioned previously that disabled youth often see the adults who surround them as being the ones who emphasize the limitations presented by their disabilities. Six teenagers who had a history of epilepsy were once entertained for a long weekend by this writer and his wife. During the course of their stay, conversation became freer as the young men and women became better acquainted with us.

Sixteen-year-old Mike commented that his parents would not ever let him ride his bicycle, although it stood in the garage unused for months at a time. He also complained that, recently, every time he made a date with a girl, his mother would call the girl's mother to tell her that Mike had epilepsy, which usually caused the date to be canceled. Criticisms against the parents began to flow so freely that with Mike's permission, the writer made an appointment with his parents and, with Mike present, visited them to explain the wide scope of activities that ought to be permitted him. At first the parents were resistant, but gradually they began to see the restrictive impact their behavior was having on Mike, particularly when reminded that Mike's medication was obviously working, and that he had not had a seizure for more than two years. In another few weeks Mike legally would not be considered epileptic, although medication would continue. Cautiously, they began to give him more and more freedom.

We do not mean to minimize the problem at all, but to indicate that children and youth with this problem need normal community support and can usually participate in everything in which physically normal youth engage. Epilepsy, per se, is not a basis for isolation from the normal activities of childhood or adolescence.

Hearing Impairment

Various degrees of hearing loss exist within any group of hard-of-hearing children. The degree of loss, however, has no bearing on whether or not a child should be included in group activities with others who have normal hearing. If the child wears a hearing aid (sometimes two), he or she usually will be able to respond to most normal sounds in speech or in the general environment: bells, bugle calls, emergency signals. The extent to which the child or young person has been taught to read lips (sometimes referred to as "speech reading") will determine, in part, the extent to which he or she will be able to enter into conversations with others. In recent years, some children have been taught the so-called "total" method, which employs both speech and the use of signs. There is controversy regarding this approach: signing is usually easier, and speech then becomes less frequently employed. Often courses in the use of signs are offered to hearing individuals, so that they can communicate easily with the youth with a severe hearing loss or who cannot utilize the hearing aid effectively. The preadolescent frequently dotes on the use of secret language between friends. Sign language is not difficult to learn. A built-in secret language could exist, which not only satisfies the preadolescent, but also opens communication between the group and the deaf child. Rarely does the hearing loss alone constitute a reason for isolating the young person from the activities of normal childhood or adolescence.

Some "do's" and "don'ts" are important. Don't yell, assuming that volume will make it possible for the deaf child to hear better. Very loud sounds may create static in the hearing aid. Speak in a normal tone, or at best raise the voice only slightly and speak directly to the individual. Eye contact is important. Be sure the child has a spare set of batteries if she is going off on an overnight hike or a week-long expedition. Remind her to take off her hearing aid for swimming or showering. Children rarely forget, but sometimes in the excitement of the moment it does happen. At a group dining room table, the clatter of dishes and the noise of many voices may prompt the youth to turn off her aid. If she does not respond to conversation, tap her on the shoulder and be sure that, for the moment, the aid is turned on. Have her allow her friends to try on the aid, so that they learn what it is like to wear the instrument, and also can hear what happens when the volume is turned up too high, or when someone yells at the wearer. (Similarly, if the crippled child utilizes crutches or a wheelchair, let normal youth use the crutches or chair in a race to learn to understand the skills that are required to use these things effecitvely, skills the crippled youth had to learn.)

Speech for most deaf children and for some with lesser hearing impairments may lack appropriate tone qualities, inflections, and speed. It is essential that those around these children *learn to listen* and to be patient while attempting to understand the spoken language of the deaf youth. This is not difficult and usually becomes automatic within a few days or weeks. Including deaf youth into social or activity groups of hearing children often opens up a totally new speech environment and vocabulary which can be exceedingly valuable to their development. It aids in building security in dealing with new social situations and with new vocabularies. At the same time, the young person can become an active participant in the social life and activities of the group, and often can make unique contributions to it. Hearing loss is no excuse for social ostracism.

Children with Cardiac Problems

The group of children with cardiac disturbances needs cautious consideration by leaders of youth groups. If these children attend school, they are able, on the whole, to particiapte in almost any group or activity. However, it is best for the group leader to discuss the child's desire to be included in a specific group, and perhaps to have the parents ask their physician prior to a final decision. A history of cardiac disturbance is not by itself a reason for exclusion from any group. Since these children and youth have what may be called an "invisible" disability— not seen by the public as a physically limiting factor—they are sometimes misunderstood when they hold back from activities which they know are beyond them, a caution which society may view as avoidance or shyness.

Emotionally Disturbed Children

Emotionally disturbed children constitute a different kind of problem. They are children with an ongoing problem which may be dealt with in the context of a special education program in the public school or may require, in addition, some form of psychotherapy provided by the mental health system. One cannot speak of emotionally disturbed children as a group. Each one must be considered individually. Many of them can be assimilated into a community youth group with little or no disruption to the group as a whole. Some of these children are very withdrawn and will not talk or interact with other children or adults. But some have serious aggressive behavior problems and can be disruptive to the point where group morale is affected. One should never exclude these persons in an offhand manner simply because they may carry the label of emotional disturbance. A careful assessment of the situation by the group leader and the parents, perhaps with school personnel or the youth's therapist included, may be warranted. No one wants to make a mistake, particularly if the error is to the child's disadvantage.

Learning Disabilities

Since about 1960, another form of exceptionality has appeared in the professional vocabulary, namely, children with learning disabilities. These are children who carry various labels, for example, minimally brain damaged, hyperactive, brain-injured, neurologically handicapped, and many others. Often this problem is due to some sort of a neurological dysfunction which was caused before, during, or shortly after birth. Normally no gross motor problems are observed, but sometimes these children seem to be very clumsy. Their problems result in eye-hand coordination problems, auditory-motor problems, and other sensory-motor problems. These can also result in memory problems, sequencing problems, inability to differentiate figure from background, very short attention spans, and a myriad of other learning problems. These children may be of any intellectual level, and they are often good-looking and very likeable. These children need social groups. They can cause behavior problems unless the tasks set before them can result in a success experience. Hence, the leader needs to be careful in what she or he asks such a child to do. These children have had a long history of failure; the more success they can experience the better. One does not "talk down" to them, but structures an activity in advance in such a way that the child has more than a fifty percent opportunity to succeed, whether it be in reading or number concepts, in riding a bike or tricycle, weaving, washing dishes, dressing, or any other daily or social activity.

Multiple and Severe Handicaps

There is a group of children and youth who present a variety of very serious problems, both physical and intellectual. This is a group known as multiple-handicapped and/or severely mentally retarded. This group of young people will present difficult problems to any religious or youth organization if integration of the individual into a group of normal youngsters is attempted. With this group of individuals, community groups and agencies may have to "reach out" rather than to "include in." We are not suggesting that integration never works; rather we are suggesting that it is difficult and will always need careful individual assistance and monitoring.

Multiple-handicapped youth are just what the name implies — individuals who experience two or more disabilities simultaneously. Usually mental retardation is one of these disabilities, but not always. Mentally retarded, cerebral-palsied children are not uncommon. Blind cerebral-palsied children are frequently encountered. Epilepsy and mental retardation often go together. (At the same time, intellectually average as well as gifted cerebral-palsied individuals live to make significant contributions to society.) Learning disabilities are often observed in children with emotional disturbances, dyslexia, aphasia, mental retardation, cerebral palsy, or in some other disability groups. Multiple disabilities can be as varied as the possibilities are varied. Every such individual will need special consideration and assistance in planning appropriate programs. No group generalizations can honestly be made.

Communication Problems

Another highly heterogeneous group of children with special needs is made up of those with speech and communication problems. The list of specific clinical problems which may be found in this group of exceptional children is long. Most commonly found are those with cleft palate, delayed speech, stuttering and stammering, and language disturbances directly related to learning disabilities, auditory perceptual problems, or to hearing loss. Such specific conditions as childhood aphasia will also be included in this category of childhood disabilities. It is estimated that this group of children constitutes between four and seven percent (depending on the inclusiveness of the definition) of the elementary school population.

Often also included in this group of children are increasing numbers of young people for whom English is a second language, including Hispanic children, children of Haitian, Vietnamese, and other refugee groups, and children of foreign nationals temporarily living in the U. S., such as university students. These children, however, do not present disabilities just because they have a primary language other than English, at least not in the same sense as those with communication problems due to emotional, neurological, or developmental factors. All of these children can with considerable ease be integrated into normal youth groups and activities.

Children with Special Health Problems

This category of problems related to childhood can be very lengthy and does include a wide variety of childhood illnesses and diseases, none of them contagious nor the basis for depriving a child of normal childhood or youth social activities. Included within this group (by way of example only, for an inclusive list would be prohibitively long) is the child with diabetes. Here it is important to the youth leader to know what medication the child may be receiving, and to be sure that someone has been designated to see that the child receives the medication if, for example, the group activity involves an away-from-home overnight camping trip. With the great majority of children in this category, the youth leader may wish to have a physician's letter of explanation regarding whatever cautions may be appropriate. Hemophilia, as another example, is a bleeding condition, and youth leaders need to know what to do if the child gets cut or falls and bleeding begins. The fact of hemophilia itself, however, is not a reason for the exclusion of a child from normal childhood activities. Tuberculosis used to be the reason for large public school programs for children with special health problems. These have largely been discontinued due to the advances in modern-day medicine. Children with acute tuberculosis should be included in general youth activities only with the advice of a physician. Often, as with severely disabled children, this will be a group of young people who will benefit from outreach programs sponsored by religious or youth groups until such time as the child can be integrated into the regular group activities. Children with asthma, chronic mild heart disease, dietetic problems, allergies, and many other chronic health problems can, with the advice of the physician, be included in most youth activities of the synagogue or church, preschool, scouts, and other formal school and youth groups. These children insofar as possible need the advantages of social contacts with their age peers; they need to learn to swim, to dance, and to engage in all of the normal activities of childhood and adolescence.

The Gifted Child

Gifted children usually are those who obtain I.Q. scores above 125 on an individual intelligence scale. They can score much higher. Frequently, because of their greater-than-average intelligence, they are able to assimilate things much more rapidly than the "normal" children with whom they associate. Often they are misunderstood by their peers. Frequently, their interests are channeled in a way that isolates them from school-aged children. Thus they need opportunities for socialization. The writer is reminded of a boy with an extraordinarily high intelligence level. At ten, he read Latin and Greek fluently. The writer, as a graduate student, was employed by the parents to do anything he could with the boy that was not academically oriented, and to get him into social groups as much as possible. This was easier said than done. Finally, by having him invite a friend to go on a hike, to go to the circus, to camp overnight in the woods, to go swimming, or to engage in other activities that he had to plan, he found that he not only enjoyed these experiences, but he could understand others and they him. Entrance into a local YMCA activity group was the next step.

Isolation or self-isolation is a most significant issue with this group; social isolation becomes a consequence of intellectual isolation. The stereotype of the bookworm, the child with horn-rimmed glasses, the quiet one, the snob—none of these need be accurate descriptions of the individual in question. To the contrary, when there is a veneer of scholarliness there is also usually a rich and inventive mind which can contribute a great deal to the activities of the group. Skilled musicianship may be appropriately exploited. Creative artistry with paints, choreography, engineering, science, and skills in other disciplines or interests may add to the richness of the social group, provided that careful leadership is employed by the adult, and the gifted child is not permitted to dominate. He or she must learn to live with others of lesser abilities and to value the contributions of each person in the group.

EXCEPTIONAL CHILDREN AS A MINORITY GROUP

In recent years, much has been written and said regarding black citizens as a minority group in the United States. Blacks and other minorities, including Native Americans and citizens of Japanese; Hispanic and other origins, have experienced rejection and have been ostracized for many decades. Practically everything which has been stated regarding racial or ethnic minorities can also be applied to the disabled population.

Because average, physically normal individuals rarely have had the privilege of associating with disabled people, they do not understand this minority group of often remarkable persons. When people, for whatever reason, do not understand, they are likely to reject. The rejection may be on the basis of fear, guilt, the appearance of the individual, because of historical or religious beliefs, or for a myriad of other real or imagined causes. Community living centers for young retarded adults have sometimes been bombed, had their windows broken or been destroyed by fire before occupancy. When government prevails and residents are actually established in a home and have lived there for a while, neighbors come to realize that the new residents are civil, pleasant, and usually happy. They maintain the lawns well, plant gardens, and in other ways meet the neighborhood standards for social acceptance. Often they are then welcomed into the neighborhood activities, occasionally even being paid to serve as baby-sitters or companions to younger children. They frequently obtain jobs in the community and contribute to their own support. They pay taxes.

In one community, a group of well-adjusted retarded adults was accepted into a neighborhood residential setting, but were refused tickets to use the city transportation system and the town swimming pool! Ultimately, their neighbors took the initiative to rescind these prohibitions. The tales of injustices rendered against these minorities are long and are a sad chapter in the social history of the United States.

These youth or adult citizens have all the legal rights of any citizen to participate fully in the life of a community and to enter appropriately into the activities of childhood and adolescence with others of their age group. Religious, educational, and youth activity groups of a community must open their doors and expand their horizons to include the disabled individual. There can be no "Jim Crow" attitude permitted in any community toward these people. The thoughtful leadership of every community must step forward and gently foster a program of integration of the disabled into the total community life. Only in this way can their minority status evaporate in meaningful ways and these citizens be provided their rightful place and birthright in our society.

PUBLIC LAW 94-142

In the mid-1960s, groups of educators, politicians, and parents, realizing that disabled children were not always receiving the educational opportunities that they deserved, began agitating for programs that would bring these children more nearly into the mainstream of public education. Chief among these groups were the U. S. Office of Education, the Council for Exceptional Children, the Education Subcommittee of the United States Senate under the leadership of Senator Edward Kennedy, as well as other individuals and organizations. *Mainstreaming, normalization* of educational opportunities, and *integration* of disabled children into ordinary classes in the community schools became watchwords. While few can yet claim outstanding examples of success with these programs, extraordinary efforts are being made to accomplish the intent of P.L. 94-142. This law is backed up by legislation at the state level and by local school district regulations. Many errors have been made, but efforts in the right direction are the general rule.

We mention this as a conclusion to this chapter because, inasmuch as public education is moving to normalize access for disabled children and youth, so must religious groups, youth organizations, and organizations such as the Ys which depend in large part upon public subscription for their support. Disabled children are with us, and so they will be for many years to come. Poliomyelitis has been virtually eradicated, thanks to the Salk and Sabin vaccines. However, cerebral palsy, birth injuries, congenital malformations, and brain injuries are still largely impervious to preventive measures. Drugs, rubella (German measles), and many childhood diseases (to say nothing of accidents) still produce a great number of handicapping conditions and leave children and young people with varying types and degrees of disability. These children and youth can no longer be isolated; they belong in life's mainstream. Community groups and organizations, in addition to the schools, must rise to the occasion and meet this nationwide challenge.

3
Families of Handicapped Children

James L. Paul

EACH FAMILY has its own strengths and resources, hopes and dreams, problems and needs. There are big families and small ones, relatively stable and well-integrated families, and some that are chaotic and disorganized; there are families that are happy most of the time, and some that are most often unhappy and sad. There are families with normally developing, healthy children, and some with children who need special attention and care. No two families are alike. Each family, with or without a handicapped child, is unique and has its own particular needs, as well as abilities to meet those needs.

There is no "typical" family of a handicapped child. Families of handicapped children have in common only the additional pressures imposed on family life by the presence of the handicapped child. The handicapped child and the family interact, each affecting the growth and development of the other. The interactive nature of child and family development exists whether or not a handicapped child is present. If a handicapped child is present, the experiences may be qualitatively different, with different demands on the family and different opportunities for growth.

While much of the focus of this chapter is on problems and negative experiences, not all family life experiences involving handicapped children are negative. The impact, whether positive or negative, varies with individual families and depends on both the child and the family.

In this chapter we will consider first the nature of the family, particularly in relation to its function in rearing children. We will consider the social pressures on family life and the stages of family development. Using this general understanding of families as a background, we will consider the development of the families of handicapped children. We will examine the demands on these families that go beyond those placed on other families, including their special difficulties in obtaining appropriate services for their children. The impact of handicapped children on different families will be discussed. Finally, some ideas for helping these families will be presented.

THE NATURE OF THE FAMILY

The family is the most basic social unit in our society. Our society depends on the family as a social institution to perform certain roles that are necessary to the stability and survival of the society. Our economic system is tied to the concept of a household. Our laws and our sociopolitical system are keyed to the rights and responsibilities of families.

There are many different views of the family and different values about the structure and functions of the family. Whatever one's views and values, however, in our society it is recognized that one of the primary roles of the family is to rear children. The values of the past are conveyed to children in the family, so that tomorrow's world will have within it what we believe is of lasting value and importance.

How does this work? One of the basic ways children learn is by imitating their parents. Children learn to talk, to behave in certain ways, and to value certain things and devalue others, by watching and listening to the way others do it. The first and most important models they have are parents.

Parents not only teach by the way they talk and act, they teach by selectively rewarding and punishing the child. That is, parents reward acceptable behavior and ignore or punish unacceptable behavior, which is a basic and effective strategy for teaching.

Parents teach skills as well as cultural values. They teach their children how to do things—how to tie shoelaces, how to dress, how to sit still and listen, how to eat, how to do simple arithmetic, and sometimes how to read. Some of this, of course, is taught by older siblings. Parents, or older siblings, also teach facts about things—about age and birthdays, holidays, about religion, and the facts about life.

Parents, of course, don't think about all of this ahead of time, and they don't have a written or memorized curriculum. They don't necessarily have a conscious commitment to a specific teaching strategy.

They usually teach what they were taught in the manner in which they were taught, although as life styles change dramatically, there may be conscious decisions to change child-rearing practices in some families.

The teaching-learning process is complex, and it involves more than just the parent and child. It typically involves two parents, each occupying a different sex role in the culture and each having different roles in the socialization of the child. The role of each parent will usually change over time as the child's needs change. Siblings are also a part of this teaching-learning transaction when they are present in a family. Extended family members such as grandparents, uncles, cousins, close friends, and neighbors also have important roles.

Each parent has a cultural blueprint for raising children etched in his/her own experiences. Some people are better at parenting than others, but most mothers and fathers do the very best they can with their physical, psychological and social resources and the training they have had.

Good times and bad times occur in the normal course of family life. Good times reassure us that we are okay; bad times and crises threaten us. Success in socially desirable activities leads to a positive self-concept. Failure can lead to self-doubt and low self-esteem. Many of an individual's psychologically important successes and failures occur or are shared in the context of a family.

While not all families have close relationships, for most of us the family is our psychological home base. The family "nest" is where one receives psychological support and instruction in the culture necessary for social and spiritual development, as well as the physical nourishment necessary for bodily growth and development. This is the laboratory where we learn if we are good and what we are good for.

This is not a one-way street. We learn from our parents and we teach our children, but our children, in turn, tell us about ourselves as parents. We learned when we were children what parents should be like. When we grow up, we try to be good parents based on our experiences, and our children tell us how well we are doing by the quality of our relationships with them and by their conformity to our understanding of good behavior for children. We learn to take credit when things work out well for our children and feel we have failed when things don't work out so well for them.

Children usually have a special regard for their parents and want to be like them. Children practice the role they hope to have someday by "playing house." Children play at being parents for their dolls and sometimes for each other. When children grow up and become parents themselves, their pretending and playing "as if" is over. When they were children, the doll or the pretend baby was exactly the way the little "mother" and "father" wanted it to be. The doll responded to the "parent's" wishes and made no uninvited demands. Unfortunately, in the real world of parenting things don't work out exactly this way. Children don't necessarily behave exactly the way we want them to. They do make demands, sometimes beyond what we are willing or even able to meet. They don't take our needs and convenience into account. Yet succeeding in the real-world parent role is very important. Being an adequate or good parent is inseparably linked with being an adequate or good person. It consists of being responsible and doing "what you are supposed to."

Being a parent is hard work for most people. To be sure, it has its psychic and spiritual rewards, but these sometimes come as by-products, delightful surprises, and long-term dividends. Meanwhile, the family must cope with considerable social pressure in its struggle to be a stable institution in the society and a positive force in the lives of its members.

THE PRESSURES ON THE FAMILY

Families today are under great stress. Grandparents and other relatives frequently are not available to help out and provide ongoing support. Neighbors do not "know each other's business" and consider it improper to inquire. Close friends are just as likely to be in the next town or the next state as they are to be next door.

Drug and alcohol abuse, teenage pregnancies, and too-early marriages impose extraordinarily heavy burdens on some families. Some people argue that these major social problems, which cut across all social strata, are symptomatic of breakdowns in family life. The cause of these problems are not simple and clear cut; neither is it clear what can be done to bring about positive change.

The traditional family structure is being challenged. The divorce rate (51% in 1978) is an indicator of how the battle is going. Alternative living arrangements, trial "marriages" and other social innovations may be viewed as adaptations to a breakdown in family life. Whether one is sympathetic to or rejects these alternatives is a matter of individual values and perspectives; but that these alternatives represent rather significant changes in the traditional nature of the family is a point on which most could agree. When special needs arise, such as the birth of a handicapped child, young parents without the presence and support of relatives and close friends in a stable community, can have a very difficult time.

Economic pressures and changes in traditional sex roles in our society have resulted in more mothers working. When you consider the number of single parent families and the families where both parents work (50.9% in 1979), and you couple this with family mobility, lack of community roots, a shortage of suitable parent substitutes who will look after the children while the parents are away, you have a situation in which many children spend a lot of time alone, and a lot of time with other children without adult supervision. When you add to this the fact that schools seem to be pretty unhappy places for many children — where the dropout rate in 1980 was over 13 percent, where some appear to be out of control, and the teacher spends most of his/her time as a disciplinarian with relatively little time left over for teaching; where many teachers are frightened, and children report being afraid to walk down the halls—you have a social picture of some concern.

A major share of responsibility for rearing and socializing children has been assumed by public agencies and institutions during the past twenty years. Day care centers for many young children bear a large responsibility for helping these children develop social and other readiness skills to prepare them for public schools. The placement of very young children, especially infants, can affect the normal psychological bonding between the infant and mother. This can be a source of stress not only in terms of the child's development, but also for the mother, who may resent having to work and, because of her economic circumstances, being virtually taken from her child.

Historically, a very important ally of the family in socializing children and teaching values has been the religious community. In our highly mobile society, where many families lack roots in the community, a church or synagogue might be one of their focal points for family life and activities. It might be the only source of roots in the community. It might become the caring community, where intimacy is possible and support is available. Unfortunately, there is little evidence that religious institutions are meeting this need at a level commensurate with the opportunity.

FAMILIES OF HANDICAPPED CHILDREN

Simeonsson and Simeonsson (1981) present an excellent discussion of the many ways in which the development of children interacts with the development of families. In the discussion that follows, their analysis is used as a primary reference.

The impact of a handicapped child on the family depends on a lot of things. The nature of the child's handicap, the severity of the handicap, and the age and sex of the child affect the child's needs and interactions with the family. The nature of the impact also has to do with factors other than the child. These include, for example, the age of the parents, the psychological resources of the family, the financial resources of the family, the values and beliefs of the family, the lifestyle of the parents, the number of siblings and the quality of their development, and the intellectual resources and information available to the parents. The nature of the community in which the family lives, the relevant personal and professional resources, and the services and supports available to the family are also important in determining the impact of a handicapped child on a family. Very important support can be provided, for example, by extended family members, religious organizations, and community groups such as the Scouts, the Ys, and social clubs that are open to the family or to individual members of the family, including a handicapped child.

The impact of a handicapped child on a family, and a family on a handicapped child, can best be understood in terms of the *interactions* within the family. To try to understand the handicapped child outside the context of the family, or the behavior and interests of parents apart from the stimulus provided by the child, is like looking at a balloon with all of the air taken out. Family life is interactive and dynamic. To take only a piece of it—a single episode, or the behavior of an individual—out of the context of the family's history and the present circumstances can be very misleading. This is just as true for a family with a handicapped child as it is for a family without a handicapped child.

CRISES IN DEVELOPMENT

The first stage of family development*—marriage—is much the same for all families. A couple is married with all of the hopes and dreams,

*For a discussion of family development, see M. A. Solomon, 1973.

expectations and fears that normally accompany the beginning of a family. The difference comes with the birth of a handicapped child.

The First Crisis

The birth of a handicapped child can be a devastating experience for parents. Solnit and Stark (1961) equated this experience with a mourning reaction on the part of the parents, who had lost an expected healthy child and realized the fear of bearing a damaged child. Olshansky (1962) described the response of parents to the knowledge that their child was mentally retarded, and would never become an independent adult, as one of chronic sorrow. This is a time of many mixed feelings for parents, including fear, sadness, and sometimes embarrassment and anger. It can be a very lonely time. The following examples (Paul and Beckman-Bell 1981) will illustrate the intensity and complexity of feelings that are involved.*

When Sara was born, her condition was totally unexpected. I had had a normal pregnancy with no records of any drugs. She was our third child and was born one day late, with a normal delivery.

In 1953, mothers were heavily drugged, and I did not know of her arrival or condition until the next day. Our obstetrician told my husband and advised him to go home for the rest of the night. She was born at 11:30 P.M.

When I woke the next morning (I had been given an injection to keep me sleeping through the night, with the approval of my husband), I was disappointed that he was not with me as he always had been before. The nurse beside me said he was unusually tired and they sent him home, that he would be back around 9.

In answer to my questions, she said we had a daughter, that she had a good strong heartbeat and lusty cry. Around 9:00, our pediatrician passed my door rather hurriedly. He did this several times, and I couldn't get his attention. I asked the nurse to tell him to come; he knew about my pregnancy and had been asked to check when the baby was born. I couldn't understand his not coming in.

Finally he did, followed by the nurse who held Sara. He said, "Mrs. D., your baby is not all right," and at that moment the nurse unwrapped her. She had on only a diaper. I reached for her and held her tightly to me, weeping, sobbing, crying.

*The examples provided here are not intended to be in any sense typical, but rather to illustrate issues in the experiences of some families.

He tried to loosen my arms, telling me I would hurt her. Almost at the same time as this (I believe they were lined up outside the door), my husband came in, followed by two of our obstetricians. They were all kind and gentle (the medicos).

The obstetrician said he would have an orthopedist—the new one in town, and only one, to come in the late afternoon—that with my consent he would like to give me another injection so I could gain strength. He promised, along with all the others, that the best care would be given to Sara. Once I had assurance, all I wanted was escape.

One card I received in the hospital (when Sara was born) meant more to me than others. It was a congratulatory baby card; but at the bottom, "We are thinking of you." I resented those who sent sympathy cards and was grateful for the few baby cards I got.

Few people sent anything, however, except flowers. They didn't know what to do. People who visited were too sympathetic, and I spent my time trying to encourage them—that we didn't know what we would do, but somehow each day would take care of itself.

Parents go through a process of adapting to the knowledge that their child is handicapped. Drotar and others (1975) identified five stages of reaction. These included shock, followed by denial, then sadness and anger, followed by adaptation and finally reorganization. This is not unlike the process of adjusting to the knowledge of death. What is involved here is the parents giving up certain hopes and dreams for their child.

It is difficult to draw in the reins on our dreams for our children, especially when we are expected to take it in all at once and adjust to the news, "your child is severely retarded," or "your child has a severe birth defect and will never be able to walk." Whether it concerns blindness, deafness, slowness, physical incapacity, or any other limiting factor, when the news is about our child and we are helpless to change the fact that he/she may never become a normally functioning independent adult, the meaning of our whole world is challenged. If our faith can be shaken, it will. If there is a weakness in our psychological armor, it is likely to surface now.

The news must be incorporated, and life in the family must go on. Families discover that their world has not come apart; it just felt that way.

It is important to recognize that this process, which varies with individual parents and families, may last for some time. Also the process is not necessarily completed, never to be revisited. The process of grieving, while it may be dealt with in a very adaptive way, is quite likely to resurface at various times throughout the child's life, as the parents experience the reality of their child's limitations and differences at each stage of development.

It is important to point out here that parents do not always become aware of a serious handicap in their child at the time of birth. For most handicapped children, the handicap is not obvious. The parents learn about most handicaps later, when the child does not grow and develop physically, socially, emotionally or intellectually as other children, or when the child is brought into situations with his or her normal peers, such as nursery school or the public school system, in which any differences and difficulties become apparent.

When knowledge of a child's handicap comes later in life, the experience will be different. The parent has already established a clear relationship with the child and knows a lot about the child. Sometimes finding out the nature of a problem that has persisted over time and even being able to give it a name can be helpful.

> Discovering the epilepsy was a great relief to me, since we had suspected it and were hoping for some explanation for Beth's condition. Emotional life for her was a shambles, causing all of us grief and turmoil. Her brother resented her for increasingly irrational and antisocial behavior. We were all distraught over her despondency and negativity. Much of this was related to puberty but seemed greatly disproportionate. Relatives and peers were alienated — she had few friends and was withdrawn and morose.
>
> She is greatly improved in all respects, due in part to the medication, partly to our understanding and relaxation, partly to growing up.
>
> I have new respect for her, as she had coped all that time alone and unaided (diagnosis of epilepsy was not reached until age 14). I am much more relaxed with her and myself, now that there is a label—an explanation for some of her discomfiting behavior. I don't feel so much distress toward any of her disruptive or antisocial behavior.

A label is not always helpful and, in fact, can present complicating difficulties. Some labels such as "mentally retarded" may be more difficult for parents to accept than other labels, such as "learning disabled." Even when labels are accurate, which is not always the case, they may not be particularly helpful in suggesting what is to be done to help the child.

The Second Crisis

The second major crisis period is when the child becomes eligible for educational services (McKeith, 1973). At this time the child's limitations become a more more public matter. No matter how protected at home during the early growth period, the child is now taking a major step out into the real, sometimes cold and sometimes cruel world. Some schools are more sensitive and better prepared to incorporate handicapped children into meaningful educational programs than others.

A parent of a physically handicapped child reported:

Sara began to feel stress because of pressure to finish on time. It was not possible for her; so each day she stayed in after school. Finally, after Sara had agonized over the problem some two to three weeks, and on a day when I waited outside for her one and a half hours, I went in and talked with the teacher.

When she realized that it was not possible for Sara to keep up, tears came in her eyes. She called Sara forward (Sara was in the back of the room trying to finish the written work), apologized, and told her that henceforth she would only do as much as she could and do it neatly, not sloppily, in order to finish on time.

She told me that since Sara would have to live in a normal world, she felt normal requirements should be made for her. I explained that some concessions would have to be made to Sara all her life, but Sara would take no more than necessary. The teacher was heartbroken that she had caused Sara to think less of school because she couldn't keep up. Awareness made the difference, and this teacher is now a principal—and I am sure a very good one. She simply thought she was doing best for Sara, when physically she was asking the impossible.

A parent of a child with epilepsy had a less fortunate experience:

The only school representative I've talked with so far was a busy counselor. She was sympathetic but also ignorant and uninformed, as I was. Her referring to the seizures as "fits" was disturbing to me and I became defensive and apologetic, for which I was later resentful. She relayed the information I gave her to the principal and teachers, but I noticed no improvements in teacher-Beth relationships or signs of support. However, neither was I aware of any negative repercussions or stigma.

A parent of a seriously emotionally disturbed child reported:

Teachers (kindergarten and the first two grades) were very supportive, worked hard with Amy, accepted her, disabilities and all. So did her first two teachers where we currently live. Then she hit the fourth-grade teacher who had no patience with even minor deviance, much less major.

In fact, that year she got two of them, one of whom spanked her— not for misbeahvior, not for not doing her homework, but *for doing the wrong homework*. I still hate myself that I did not sue.

The Third Crisis

The third crisis period identified by McKeith is when the handicapped child leaves school. This may be a time for which the parents have planned, or it may be a time of major concern and even mild panic. The child is now older, physically more mature, and his or her needs as an individual have changed. Depending on the handicapping condition, going to college and/or entering the normal work force may or may not be out of the question. Parents are often without the information they need about opportunities for their child at this period.

During this period, the normal family process would involve the young person's beginning to give up his or her own family as a source of primary gratification and starting to develop other bases for primary gratification. This is not the case for many of these children and their families.

The Fourth Crisis

The final crisis identified by McKeith involves the time when the parents are aging and can no longer assume primary responsibility for their handicapped offspring. The parents must adjust to their own aging and make adjustments to the special arrangements that may be necessary for their offspring.

In summary, then, there are four major crisis periods in the development in the lives of families with a handicapped child. This perspective helps us understand how the needs of families change. It is important to understand where families are and what they are facing in order to be able to offer meaningful support and assistance.

ADDITIONAL DEMANDS

Families of handicapped children must adjust to many demands not a part of the lives of most families.* Depending on the nature of the child's handicap, the family may have to deal with thoughtless ridicule or curiosity on the part of others, and with long, expensive, and sometimes frustrating and even hurtful experiences with hospitals and many professionals. The story of how a severely handicapped child can affect the life of a family is sensitively told by Ann Turnbull in Chapter One.

Two of these major special demands will be discussed here. The first has to do with the special relationship between a parent and a child as the child grows and develops, and the ways that relationship can be affected by the child's handicap. The second involves the process of getting appropriate professional services for the child, and the possibility of being treated as the cause of the child's problem. Both of these special demands on parents reflect the fact that the stigma of a handicap is shared by the family. The parent of a retarded child, a child with epilepsy, an autistic child, or a child with any other handicapping condition shares the stigma our society associates with that particular handicap.

Parent–Child Relationships

Children normally identify with their parents and become a source of great pride to them. These feelings of pride are rewarding to the parents and reinforce the parents' interactions with the child and result in the parents' being even more active in the child's life. Unfortunately, this process is short-circuited in the development of many handicapped children. Some parents of handicapped children denied the satisfaction of these needs. Rather than being sources of joy and pride, their children sometimes act in public in ways that are embarrassing and can be experienced as humiliating. This is a painful experience, and it is normal to try to avoid or reduce pain. These experiences will discourage the parent from taking the child into situations where the parent may be embarrassed, and they reduce the likelihood that, given the option, the parent will choose to spend time with the child.

*For a more detailed discussion of the demand on families of handicapped children, the reader is referred to Travis (1976), Battle (1974), and Simeonsson and Simeonsson (1981).

Thus, they will tend to reduce the amount and the quality of time the parent and the child spend together.

Children are immensely gratified when they can please their parents. The parents are gratified, and their good feelings, satisfaction and approval of a child's behavior give strength to the behavior and increase the chances for similar behavior in the future. This is a closed circuit. The parent feels something like, "I am pleased with you and approve of your behavior. I know that my approval is important to you; I am a good parent and we are a good family"; and the child in turn perceives, "I am pleased, I have pleased you, and I must be doing okay." This is the circuitry of success. It is the chemistry of ego development— both the ego of the child and the parent ego.

With the seriously handicapped child, one is likely to find a break in this circuit. Much of life is made up of failure experiences, in which neither the child nor the parent gains approval from the other. Messages of, "I am not pleased or pleasing to you; I am not okay; we are not okay" can dominate the family experience. This translates into, "I am not loved, therefore, I am not lovable." This same negative circuit of failure experiences, disappointment, anger, sadness, resentment, and more failure experiences also often works between the handicapped child and siblings. This dynamic can color and dominate family interactions.

The amazing thing is that families can gain insight into these dynamics and, as an act of love, will intervene to change them. Parents and siblings alike choose to take risks. These families are often required to dig much deeper inside themselves for resources with which to cope with their circumstances than most families do. Most often they find those resources and sometimes become champions of the cause of the handicapped, working not only for the interest of their own child, but for other handicapped children as well. Many of these families find support groups in religious groups or with other families of handicapped children.

These parents learn that their child is an individual in his or her own right, and they cannot be responsible for their child's behavior any more than other parents can be responsible for the behavior of their children. These parents often come to expect success in spite of past experiences and regard their child as an individual with dignity and rights of his or her own. One parent recently commented to me, "I felt very good the day I decided I would never again apologize for Bill's behavior. I just don't apologize any more, because I realized that he is not me and I am not responsible. I have not done anything wrong for which I should be apologizing." This kind of separation of self from the child's handicap is necessary, especially when the parent seeks help for the child. This issue is discussed in the following section.

Getting Appropriate Services and Dealing with Guilt

Unfortunately, it is very difficult for families to get the information, counseling and support they need without paying a heavy price for it. Sometimes it is indeed a high financial price, and parents are drained of their financial resources by expensive treatment that may or may not be effective or even needed. However, there are other costs associated with gaining the support they need. Often parents go to a professional helping system; such as the mental health system or a hospital, and are treated as if they were the problem. Parents are already hurt, tired and often understandably angry about their situation. Often they are haunted by the fear that they are in some way responsible for what has happened. If not their "bad genes" or the bad decisions they made during the pregnancy, then the problem, they fear, may be the result of their having been inadequate parents. What parents of normal children have not wondered about themselves when their offspring got into trouble? After all, "This is my flesh and blood, and I raised him/her; where did I go wrong?"

For many parents the jury is in; they have judged themselves guilty and bear the burden of feeling responsible. But the fact is that human behavior is extraordinarily complex, and it is very rare when simple cause and effect relationships can be established. Even though all parents make mistakes, they do the best they can given the emotional, social, cultural and financial resources available to them.

Behavior is interactive. We went through a period of time when professionals thought mental retardation was primarily an organic problem resulting from biological or genetic factors. This was later replaced by the equally appealing view — appealing from the perspective of research evidence available at the time—that mental retardation was the result of environmental factors. Now, on the basis of evidence available at the present time, it seems relatively clear that mental retardation is a complex problem of intelligence and adaptive behavior which results from an interaction over time of organic factors within the child and environmental factors outside the child.

A similar problem has existed in understanding the cause of autism. We went through a long period of time when much of the blame was focused on mothers who were labeled "refrigerator mothers" and considered unresponsive to their autistic children. More recent research has pointed out that infants have profound effects on the behavior of parents, especially their mothers, who are typically their primary care givers. It has been recognized that the responses of the mother and father could just as well be conditioned by the behavior of an autistic infant who fails to respond to normal parental behavior, as much as the behavior of infants could be related to the attitudes, behavior, and disposition of the parents. In fact, results of recent research have placed more emphasis on the organic developmental component of autism than on the environmental aspect.

As best we can tell at the present time, given that our sciences of behavior are still at a relatively primitive level of development, behavior is the result of interactions over time between the genetic capacity of the child and the environment. The environment must teach and stimulate growth. The capacities of children to use education and stimulation and to grow vary; some are more limited than others. Similarly, the resources of environments vary widely; some environments are more stimulating and rich in educational value than others. The spoken language to which a child is exposed over time, the attitudes of those around him or her, the written materials available, the expectation of significant others in the environment, the emotional quality and tone of the environment, the food available, medical care, consistency—these and many other factors interact to comprise an environment which either facilitates or impedes the growth and development of the child.

Not only is it technically in error for parents to assume the responsibility for having caused the child's problem, or to view the child as the victim of their mistakes, it is a guilt trip that takes energy. It is a waste of energy to "beat oneself over the head" with guilt, when that energy could be going into planning and implementing a positive experience.

Human services are arranged in such a way that when parents go to get help, they sometimes get the message that they are the problem and they become the focus of treatment. Unfortunately, many professionals still operate this way.

While they are not necessarily the cause of their child's problem, it is certainly true that the dynamics and difficulties of families with a handicapped child can so drain the psychological resources of the family, lower self-esteem, and reduce the ability of parents to function productively, that supportive counseling may be in order. Marriages can get in trouble in the midst of these crises, and marriage counseling is sometimes needed. One parent recently said to me, "You have to have a strong marriage to make it through this; it is amazing how many don't make it."

Parents will often lash out at each other when their real anger is at the child, or when they are simply frustrated with not knowing which way to turn. The attacked parent may not have the ego resources to absorb the anger and frustration of the mate. Also, there are legitimate differences between parents regarding how best to approach care for the child. For example, one parent may want to keep the child as much in the mainstream with nonhandicapped children as possible. The other parent may want to protect the child and have him or her in a more protected setting, such as a special class. One parent may want to keep the child at home, while the other parent believes the child should be in an institution. One parent may be optimistic about possibilities and actively seek alternatives, while the other parent is less optimistic and is willing to accept what is known to be available and has been recommended. Both parents want the very best for their child, and both of them have found or are looking for the best services for their child. They are also coping with the hurt and disappointment of this experience. Several professionals have noted that the presence of a handicapped child can strengthen a marriage and bring spouses closer together (Burton, 1975). It is important also to recognize that the stress can become too much and result in divorce.

There are several factors that affect the impact of a handicapped child on the family. In the following section some of these will be described.

Experiences of Parents with Professionals

Feelings of parents about professionals and their experiences with them are mixed. The following examples illustrate difficulties some parents have had getting appropriate services for their child and the feelings that resulted. Each parent quoted here had both good and bad experiences.

A parent of a multiply handicapped boy wrote:

Professionals, including school personnel, have most often seemed to me to be primarily concerned with the comfort and safety of the organizations they serve. Many such professionals told me that they could not serve my son because he would not fit within their program.

In addition, there seemed to be an unwillingness of staff to accept the parent as a partner in working with the developmentally disabled child.

A mother of a physically handicapped girl wrote:

The door opened and the room became crowded with med students, male and female, who watched and listened as Dr. R. examined our naked baby and told of her condition. She screamed the entire time and he handled her as coldly as an object, and his words were just as cold. Then they started out. I stopped Dr. R. and asked his advice to us. "A full report will go to your doctor," he said, and left.

Sara was then taken, naked, by a male attendant and held up before a camera, still crying, for pictures from all directions. Neither we nor our doctor ever had any reports, and this was a terrible experience. Sara was not treated as a human being but an object, and we as well, or as nonpersons.

This same mother told of another experience.

Now, for the bad experience: We were sent to a local surgeon for his opinion (of my daughter's reports of pain which had resulted in her having to miss school). He said it was psychosomatic, that she had created a cycle of pain and tension (they had given her many drugs to relax her), and that in order to break it he wanted to put six injections—three on each side of the top area of the stomach between the breastbone (where a hiatal hernia would be)—of morphine.

This would break the cycle and it would all be over. Sara was on the table and screamed and pleaded not to be given the shots. My husband and I both talked with her, encouraging her to try this one last thing, saying that, "It would hurt but try to bear it."

She still screamed no, so the doctor asked us to leave the room. We waited in his office across the hall and heard her cries and no's and screams; but at the beginning it was very quiet. She later told us that he held the needle over her and said, "If you promise me that you'll go to school tomorrow and stop all this nonsense, I will not put this shot into you." The needle was almost horse size.

She told him she couldn't promise that because she had already tried, and the temperature and pain remained and was too much. He threatened her over and over again, telling her how much it would hurt, how she could so easily promise.

This mother would have promised that, I'm afraid, but Sara would not promise what she knew she could not carry out; so he put in six big injections. Then he came to his office and told us, "Your problem is obvious. Sara is treated like a baby. You (the mother) are her problem. You hover over her and treat her like an infant. She doesn't have a chance as long as you must baby her."

This was so opposite of our situation—Sara has always been independent—and so I told him how she had stayed home by herself many days. I was floored by his charges and admit I couldn't adequately respond.

Then he said, "Perhaps the opposite is the case. Maybe she is doing this to get the love you are denying her." The nurse came out with Sara in her arms. We took her and went home, all of us feeling very dejected, but drawn closer than ever. Next day I stayed home with Sara and on impulse called to speak with Dr. A.R.S.'s successor, who also admired Sara and had encouraged us so much.

I briefly described her stomach pain, the temperature, the tests (but not our last experience—except the decision that it was psychosomatic). He said quickly, "It can't be; not Sara? Have you checked the fascia [the tissue connecting bone and muscle]?"

We took her to the orthopedist here who had helped her many times for falls, etc., and who had encouraged us many times. This had not seemed to be bone-related so we hadn't seen him. "Of course," he said after the examination, and gave Sara a drug that cleared it up completely in one week. That one telephone call to a distant doctor was all it took. Those six weeks are a horror to me, and I'm sure had a detrimental effect on Sara, although she knew we were not party to that decision (except for the six injections, which still make me cringe).

A mother of a schizophrenic girl told of being referred to many different agencies that were not at all helpful. After much expense, emotional trauma, and persistance, she found professionals willing and able to help. She reports:

A psychoeducational program for autistic children was by far the most supportive and the most helpful of the agencies from which we have sought help. Dr. Schopler and Dr. Reichler blend humility ("We don't know everything"), academic expertise, common sense, and humanity in their approach. Although Amy was both too old and too advanced for their program, they helped us work out a home program to help improve cognition, language, and behavior. I can hardly praise these two men too much.

After both good and bad experiences, this mother concluded:

From our experience with professionals, we have learned the following:

1. Never trust a professional who doesn't admit, "We don't have all the answers," and who tends to shunt parental concerns and suggestions aside.

2. If a professional is riding one particular hobby horse exclusively —i.e., Freudianism, behavior mod—he probably has blind spots that mar his competence.

3. With teachers, training in "special needs" is important; but sensitivity is more important. Same goes for psychologists and psychiatrists.

FACTORS AFFECTING THE IMPACT OF A HANDICAPPED CHILD ON THE FAMILY

In thinking about ways of understanding and being helpful to families with handicapped children, it is interesting to consider the types of family circumstances in which handicapped children are born. Stedman (1977) described nine categories of family patterns in terms of the impact handicapped children have on their families and which are relevant to treatment. These are briefly described below:

1. *Older parents.* The largest homogeneous group of mentally retarded children are those affected by Down's syndrome (mongolism). In many instances, the birth of a child with Down's syndrome appears to be associated with the age of the mother. In some cases, the birth of a handicapped child is coupled with premenopausal or midmenopausal changes in the mother and pre- or mid-climacteric change in the father. While older parents are likely to be financially more secure than younger parents, they are not necessarily better prepared to deal with the emotional impact of having a handicapped child. The kind of support needed by these parents depends on a number of things, including whether the birth was planned, the attitudes of the parents toward their handicapped infant, and their flexibility in considering child care alternatives.

2. *The isolated couple.* Sometimes a young couple is geographically isolated from their family and friends, perhaps as a result of moving to a new job or to a university to continue their education. When a handicapped child is born under these circumstances, there is a great need for emotional support. This is a situation that can threaten the integrity of the young family and can ultimately be very destructive to the marriage. Support of family and friends and special counseling and assistance are important.

3. *The professional family.* The professional family may be expected to understand and deal with the emotionally charged event of the birth of a handicapped child more objectively than other parents. This is not necessarily something they are able to do. Frequently professional parents attempt to cope with this issue in such an objective fashion that they do not deal adequately with the emotional dimensions of the experience, including their own hurt and disappointment. It is important to recognize these needs and take great care in providing support to this family. These parents need friends to "be there" and constructive channels for emotional discharge, not an eventual breakdown of their defenses that may result in depression and anger.

4. *The low-income family.* Families with little material means have less access to services for the handicapped child than do middle-income families. These parents may also have less information about handicapped children and services available to them.

5. *The disturbed family.* When problems already exist in family relationships, the birth of a handicapped child can be especially traumatic. A family that is already on shaky ground may find in the handicapped child someone on whom to blame their problems. These families need a great deal of support. Having friends available, "on call," is very important, and professional counseling is usually needed in these instances.

6. *The large family.* In some instances, the handicapped child may be the fourth, fifth, or sixth child born into the family. Large families may involve greater stresses on the parents and certainly increase the logistical problems involved in managing a large family. There are also many more relationships to consider in a large family. If the family has limited means and high stress, then the birth of a handicapped child can be especially problematic. However, if the family is well-integrated and functioning in an emotional context of openness, warmth and mutual support, and often if special support is given to the mother, a large family can create support for itself and for the handicapped child that is not available in smaller families.

7. *Single-parent families.* When couples are separated or when a handicapped child is born to a single mother, the major issue is the lack of emotional support of each parent for the other. The birth of a handicapped child can be a very lonely experience for a couple, but it is even more so when the parents are functioning as separate individuals rather than as a couple. The family of the parents may not be as available to be supportive and to be used as "shock absorbers" if they are unhappy with the parents' marital situation. In a situation of separation or divorce, the

parents are dealing simultaneously with two traumas: the birth of a handicapped child and the end of their marriage. Support of these individuals is important, based on a recognition of the additional stresses they face.

8. *The "religious" family.* There are some families who choose to view the birth of a handicapped infant as "the will of God" and take no direct responsibility for making decisions that may be needed concerning special care for the child. Religious affiliation is, in general, a positive force in preventing the disintegration of the family, but the family must be assisted in taking responsibility for making decisions for the child. The family's rabbi, minister, or priest can be especially helpful to these families.

9. *The "average" family.* While each family is unique, it is useful to think of the concept of an "average" family in the sense that a family is like the majority of families in the country in terms of income, age of parents, proximity to their family, and so forth. In families that appear to be average in most senses of the word, the impact of the handicapped child may be underestimated. Some families appear to "have it all together" and be well adjusted, when deep struggles of conscience and feelings of guilt and anger have not been dealt with. "One should not be suspicious of the family that fails to fall apart in the face of the impact of the handicapped child, but one should not be misguided by apparent family tranquility" (Stedman, 1977). It is important to be available to these families for support as needed.

HOW TO HELP FAMILIES WITH A HANDICAPPED CHILD

What should be clear from the discussion in this chapter is that all families are different and, therefore, their needs are different. It should also be clear that any family with a handicapped child does have special needs.

When considering the needs of a family and how to meet them, it may be helpful to consider what you have to offer. Do you have a long-term relationship with the family that is positive and on which they are going to need to depend at this time? Are you a relative whose opinion about the situation will be very important to the couple, and about whom they may be apprehensive? Are you part of a group of which the family is a member, such as the temple? Do you have special information about handicapping conditions in children or services available? Are you a friend who wants to help but cannot think of a specific, tangible way to be helpful? The important thing here is to think —to think about what the needs are, and to think about a way or ways in which you may help.

While it may sound cold, it is worth considering what needs and fears you may have concerning the handicapped child and the family. There is nothing wrong with needing to help. However, needing the family to help you deal with your anxiety about what is happening to them is not a legitimate basis on which to offer help.

In considering the needs of a family, it is important to remember that their needs change. It is helpful to think about the family's situation at a particular time and the kinds of needs they are likely to have. This is a good place to start in helping the family.

This doesn't mean that you must totally intellectualize your relationship with the family, or that you must be smart and figure out their needs. There is certainly no need to dazzle the family with your insight into their situation. On the other hand, there is nothing wrong with having enough regard for the family that you pause to reflect on their circumstances and needs. It is indeed the case that sometimes "fools rush in where angels fear to tread."

Another need (and right) families have is for privacy. Families need time to be alone, and they need space that is not community property. There are subjects about which you may be curious, but to inquire would be an invasion of privacy. Only your own personal sensitivity will guide you in these matters.

Professor Leo Rippy years ago taught me a very important truth about helping others. He said sometimes all you can do is "be there," but there are many times when being there is all that is needed. When parents go through the difficult process of adjustment to the reality of a seriously handicapped child in their family, they have a right to experience their feelings and a right to be free from a lot of talk, and especially free from a lot of advice from others who have never had that experience and could not possibly know their feelings and thoughts. On the other hand, even in the hardest moments—perhaps especially then—it is very important for parents to know they have people available they can call: friends who will willingly listen and care about what they are experiencing; a minister who is not frightened of what is happening to them, and who does not view their experience as a punishment from God for some wrong they have done; relatives who will not be judgmental or look down on them or reject their baby. Being there and really caring creates a psychological and spiritual lifeline for lonely and brokenhearted parents that nourishes them during a period in which they are perhaps more vulnerable than they have ever been. In time, the parents will integrate the experience into their lives, and that integration and adjustment will be much easier with a little help (or a lot of help, as the case may be) from their friends.

Parents sometimes need help in finding and maintaining hope. As their child grows into each stage of development, the parents must make decisions about what is reasonable to expect of the child and of themselves. Parents also have to deal with priorities for their family. For example, the addition of a severely handicapped child may place such additional demands on the parents, and claim so much of their energies, that their other important responsibilities—to one another or to other children in the family—may be abdicated.

Parents need the opportunity to share their experiences and to learn from others. Parents of handicapped children find a lot of support from other parents of handicapped children. This is a unique source of learning and support that probably cannot be provided by others.

Informal support networks are extremely important for parents. For example, Bristol (1979) found that the adequacy of interpersonal support systems was very important in the ability of mothers of autistic children to cope.

Afford the family the dignity of expecting from them positive adjustments and adaptations. You do the family a service by believing they have the resources necessary to cope. They do. In most instances, buoyed up by the support of friends and others, parents find within themselves and within the family the strength they need, often more than they ever dreamed they had.

What parents need more often than not is information. Sometimes they need help in understanding what is going on with their child; sometimes they need training and help in developing the skills necessary to talk with or manage the behavior of their child; sometimes they need to know how to work with others—teachers, mental health professionals, medical doctors, etc.; sometimes they need financial assistance; sometimes they need to know about services that are available for their child; sometimes they need advocates to help them and their child with a difficult situation at school, or in the home or community; sometimes they need legal counsel; sometimes they need help in planning for what is going to happen to their child when they grow older and are unable to take care of him/her; sometimes what parents need more than anything else is respite, a time when they can be alone and enjoy their privacy as a married couple.

Sometimes parents need help with major decisions. Their need may be for "another opinion," for specific information, or for someone to provide emotional support through a difficult decision that only they can make. One of the hardest decisions a family must face when they have a handicapped child has to do with institutionalization. Stedman (1977) describes three major factors connected with assisting families in their decision about institutionalization for their child. One factor has to do with the degree of distance of the family, geographically and emotionally, from potential sources of support in a situation when a decision is being made. The second factor has to do with the ability of a family to use emotional support. This may be in the form of support provided by the church, family, and friends, or through professional counseling. The third factor has to do with the extent to which a family has a supportive person available to them who can help them think objectively about the situation. This person may be the minister, the family doctor, a lawyer, an educator, or some other person who is concerned about the child and the family. Stedman warns that it is never a simple situation, where simple criteria can be applied in reaching an automatic answer to the question, "Should this child be institutionalized?" It is a very difficult and psychologically demanding process.

In most instances, institutionalization of a handicapped child is not indicated. But in some instances where a severe or profound disability is involved, and where resources in the community are limited, institutionalization may be indicated.

During the past five to ten years, there has been a rather strong move to provide services in the community to handicapped persons who were previously served in institutions. Group homes, sheltered workshops, a variety of semi-independent living arrangements, counseling, and other support services have been developed. Most of the mild-to-moderately retarded population have been moved from institutions into communities. This move to deinstitutionalize the handicapped has been based on several factors, including an emphasis on the civil rights of handicapped individuals. An institution can be a very limited living arrangement which compromises the freedom of individuals. On the other hand, the institution can provide a needed service for severely and profoundly handicapped individuals who cannot function in the community or use community services.

There are sometimes no clear-cut right or wrong decisions about institutionalization. Parents need the genuine support of others who care when they are faced with long-term decisions about their child. Institutions are placements of choice by parents when they do not see a caring and enduring community that will help with the life-long care of their child, who will age but not mature, and who will be at least partially dependent the rest of his or her life.

It may be useful to think about what these families do not need. They do not need to be excluded by architectural barriers from buildings in the community which are readily available to others. They do not need to be excluded because the curriculum in an educational program is only for the sighted, the hearing, the ablebodied and the intellectually normal. They do not need to be excluded from social gatherings "because they might bring their daughter." Shunning a child or a family because we are uncomfortable is an easy way to cope; it is also unfair to the family, and robs us of the opportunity to learn and grow.

Feelings of discomfort can be discussed with a minister, or with the parents themselves if it is done appropriately. For example, one can say, "I really don't know anything about mental retardation and I don't know exactly how best to relate to Caroline" (these children have names too, and using their names rather than "your daughter" or some other impersonal reference is helpful). It is easier to ask for information than to ask the parent to reassure you because you are uneasy or uncomfortable. The parent will usually be aware of your feeling anyway. You need not feel embarrassed to say you don't know, or that you don't understand but are interested in knowing.

It is important to be careful about the time and place you pick to find out about these things. Having the family over for a cup of coffee in your home or going to a sporting event such as a ball game together might be a good time. Try to do this at a time and during an activity in which you feel most comfortable and most confident, and where there is the least likelihood of an awkward scene. For example, it may not be a good idea to invite the family to come over for a meal and bring Caroline, as your first effort to learn more about her and her needs. An appreciated offer might be to say to parents at an appropriate time and place, "I'm interested in Caroline and perhaps there may be a time when I could babysit for you (depending on Caroline's age and needs), but I really don't know very much about deaf children. If you could tell me more about her and how I can relate to her, I would like it and perhaps I can be helpful."

Another kind of approach is to arrange to have a special program or even a short course on children with special needs conducted in the church or synagogue, or in some other community program. This can be a rewarding intellectual experience and provide the basis for getting to know members of the congregation with special needs on a more personal basis. There is usually someone in the community—a rabbi or minister; someone from the public school system, such as a special educator; someone from the university; or others—able and willing to conduct such a seminar or course. This can involve not only a discussion of the characteristics and individual needs of the handicapped, but also some discussion of the services that are available in your specific community and the services that are needed which are unavailable. This kind of study can be taken on by a church or synagogue, for example, or even by several congregations in the community as an ecumenical activity. For the members, it means some real analysis of human need and opportunities for service in the community. This can be an exciting and rewarding undertaking, in which professionals in the community get involved, as well as parents of handicapped children and parent organizations, such as the Association for Retarded Citizens, the Association for Children with Learning Disabilities, the Society for Autistic Children, the Epilepsy Foundation, United Cerebral Palsy, and others. There is considerable literature available from the offices of these national organizations. This information can be easily collected and made available for study and placed in the religious organization's library. Most of these associations have local chapters; the chapter presidents are usually glad to participate in programs of education for the community, especially those that might result in some activities on behalf of the handicapped. The national offices of these various organizations will provide you with information about organizations in your state and list the presidents of these organizations. These individuals can tell you about chapter organizations in your local area.

Families of handicapped children need positive support. They do not need sympathy. It is demeaning to feel sorry for them. To try instead to understand their feelings and what they are facing can be very helpful. Empathy is something that we all need at some time. There is an opportunity for service available to those who will take the time and the risk involved in getting to know more about the lives of these children and their families.

REFERENCES

Battle, C. "Disruptions in the Socialization of a Young Severely Handicapped Child." *Rehabilitation Literature* 35 (1974):130–40.

Bristol, M. "Maternal Coping with Autistic Children: Adequacy of Interpersonal Support and Effects of Child's Characteristics." Doctoral dissertation, University of North Carolina at Chapel Hill, 1979.

Burton, L. *The Family Life of Sick Children.* London: Routledge and Kegan Paul, 1975.

Dortar, D., Baskiewicz, A., Irvin, N., Kennell, J., and Klaus, M. "The Adaptation of Parents to the Birth of an Infant with Congenital Malformation." *Pediatrics* 56 (1975):710–17.

MacKeith, R. "The Feelings and Behavior of Parents of Handicapped Children." *Developmental Medicine and Child Neurology* 15 (1973):524–27.

Olshansky, S. "Chronic Sorrow: A Response to Having a Mentally Deficient Child." *Social Casework* April 1962, pp. 13–15.

Paul, J., and Beckman-Bell, P. "Parent Perspective." In *Understanding and Working with Parents of Children with Special Needs,* edited by J. Paul. New York: Holt, Rinehart and Winston, 1981.

Simeonsson, R., and Simeonsson, N. "Parenting Handicapped Children: Psychological Aspects." In *Understanding and Working with Parents of Children with Special Needs,* edited by J. Paul. New York: Holt, Rinehart and Winston, 1981.

Solnit, A., and Stark, M. "Mourning and the Birth of a Defective Child." In *Psychoanalytic Study of the Child,* edited by K. Eissler et al. New York: International University Press, 1961.

Solomon, M. "A Developmental Conceptual Premise for Family Therapy." *Family Process* 12 (1973):179–88.

Stedman, D. "Introduction." In *Deinstitutionalization: Implications for Policy and Program Development,* edited by G. Neufeld, J. Paul, and D. Stedman. Syracuse, N.Y.: Syracuse University Press, 1977.

Travis, G. *Chronic Illness: Its Impact on Child and Family.* Stanford, California: Stanford University Press, 1976.

4
Principles for Working with the Handicapped Child in Religious Education Programs, Youth Recreation Groups, and Other Community Settings

Grace P. Lane

RELIGIOUS EDUCATION TEACHERS and scouting and other youth program leaders are rarely professionals trained in the teaching and leadership of children. Rather, they are volunteers from a wide range of personal and educational backgrounds and occupations, whose common characteristic is the love of children and a desire to help children develop into successful, wholesome individuals. Many are parents of children who attend religious education classes, or belong to a scout troop, team, or other youth group; some are young adults who enjoy working with children and hope to become teachers, physical therapists and the like; some may be older adults whose own children are grown and who wish to renew the opportunity to share experiences with children.

Whatever their backgrounds and reasons for volunteering as teachers and youth leaders, most have had little if any formal training in working with children, and therefore approach their leadership role with a mixture of enthusiasm, uncertainty, and self-doubt. Stage fright is not at all uncommon among new leaders. They are likely to wonder about such issues as, "Will the children like me? Will they respond to me? Can I keep their behavior under control? Will the children enjoy the activities I plan?"

Such feelings and concerns are likely to be magnified to near panic if the teacher learns that his or her class will include a handicapped child. Even experienced leaders may feel inadequate to cope with a child who is "different." They may even feel some degree of resentment toward the handicapped child and toward the parents who are sending the child into an otherwise "normal" group.

It should be emphasized that these fears and resentments are quite normal. Viewing the handicapped child as a burden "above and beyond the call of duty" is not at all unusual. Many experienced, professional educators felt the same way when mainstreaming was first implemented in the public schools.

Fortunately, fears about working with the handicapped child can be quickly allayed. Handicapped children are "different" only in respect to their handicapping condition. Otherwise they are just like normal children. They enjoy learning new information and skills. They take pleasure in arts and crafts, music, poetry, stories, and games. Most of all, they enjoy being part of the group.

There are other reasons why the religious education teacher or youth leader should not be afraid of the handicapped child. First of all, most handicapped children have already been identified as such by their parents or by the school system, and are already receiving special help to overcome or adapt to the handicapping condition. The physically handicapped child as well as the child with health problems has probably been taught to recognize his or her physical limitations and abilities and is learning how to cope with them.

Secondly, the handicapped child is very likely known to some of the other members of the class or group. Most handicapped children are now attending public schools and frequently are mainstreamed into a regular classroom. They probably have several classmates in the church school group or youth group who already know them and are accustomed to interacting with them. If this is the case, the "normal" children are aware of the exceptional child's needs, limitations, and abilities. These normal classmates are usually eager to help when help is needed, and they seem to know when the handicapped child can be treated "normally." Such children can be great allies to the community group leader.

In the third place, it is frequently easy to obtain volunteer help when working with a handicapped child. Older teenagers in the church or community are often eager to assist, as are other adults who may have been reluctant to take on the role of teacher or leader themselves.

Finally, the handicapped child's parents are an invaluable source of information on how to meet their child's special needs, and may be able to refer the religious education teacher to community agencies and professionals who might be willing to provide helpful suggestions.

It should also be noted that all scouting groups and many religious education programs offer some training to the novice leader, and provide a curriculum or program guide to follow in working with the group.

Most of the training offered applies to leading exceptional as well as normal children. Such training can help the new volunteer to feel secure in his or her new leadership role. The program offered to the class or group will usually be appropriate for handicapped children as well as for their normal peers, requiring only minor adaptations, if any.

With these considerations set forth, this chapter will examine several basic principles for working with handicapped children in religious programs and other community settings. These principles include parent involvement, assessment of the child's needs, and behavior management.

PARENT INVOLVEMENT

Parents of handicapped children have already been mentioned as a source of information and assistance to the group leader. Parent involvement is not only helpful, it is absolutely essential if the children are to obtain maximum benefit from their experiences in the group. If the parents themselves do not initiate communication, the church school teacher should not hesitate to set up a conference.

Novice leaders may be reluctant to approach the parents about the child's handicap. They may be uncomfortable about the prospect of working with the child, yet do not wish to convey discomfort to the parents. They may fear that they will "say the wrong thing" and hurt the parents' feelings. If the leader is tactful, these fears are probably unfounded. Parents of handicapped children are quite accustomed to being approached for conferences. While they resent negative comments about their child (they have already heard too many), they will welcome sincere efforts to understand, accept, and assist.

While the group leader will undoubtedly want to be informed about the child's limitations—and he or she *should* be informed about them—it is best to focus on the child's positive characteristics. What *can* the child do? What does the child enjoy doing? Questions such as these help to assure the parents that the leader intends to provide the child with a fruitful experience.

One important point that should be discussed with parents is what, if anything, they would like for the child's classmates or youth group peers to know about the handicapping condition. Parents of exceptional children usually have had many experiences with introducing their offspring into a new social or academic situation. They know how other children have reacted in the past, and they probably have some definite ideas about what information will facilitate their child's acceptance into the group. They may suggest keeping their child out of the group for one meeting, so that the teacher can explain the handicapping condition to the rest of the class. The parents can frequently tell the teacher exactly what to say to the group. Most likely they will want to explain what the disability is, how it affects the child, and what other members of the class should and should not do to help. (It is important that well-meaning leaders and peers *not* do things for handicapped children that they reasonably can be expected to do for themselves.)

It is a good idea, even if the parents don't suggest it, to tell the group that the handicapped child will enjoy being part of the group and will be pleased simply to be with them.

During the initial conference with the child's parents, it is especially important to find out what the parents expect from the group. Do they want the child to learn religious stories, to make arts and crafts projects, to take part in a holiday pageant, to earn merit badges, to go on hikes? Do they want the leader to challenge their child to the limits of his or her abilities, or do they simply want to provide their child with a social experience?

Coming to a mutual agreement about goals and expectations for the handicapped child will help both teachers and parents to plan for successful experiences. For example, if the parents expect the child to learn specific information such as religious stories and doctrine, it may be necessary for them to review the lesson with the child during the week or find a tutor to supervise the review. If they expect the child to take part in a pageant or other performance, they must help to decide realistically what kind of part the child is able to play, and they will need to help the child rehearse the part until he or she is comfortable with it. Such rehearsal is essential even if the child has no lines to speak and will be standing as a shepherd in a Christmas tableau; the handicapped child needs to feel secure.

Parents of handicapped children will often stop by the religious education classroom for a few minutes after class to ask about the day's lesson. A mother of a severely hearing-impaired child who had a habit of doing this explained that her son was very interested in the lessons, especially when there were pictures, but that he missed some of the spoken lesson. He would then ask her questions when he got home, and unless she knew what had been said in class, she couldn't very well answer him.

The parents of a mentally retarded child who were diligent in obtaining the "take home" leaflet from church school pointed out that their child loved the stories, but needed many repetitions at home before he could remember them.

During the initial parent-teacher conference, the teacher should be told whether the child is on medication for hyperactivity, seizures, diabetes, or the like. The parents should explain the effects of the medication, and should alert the teacher to the symptoms of any possible reactions. The teacher should be informed about what to do in case the symptoms develop. (This point is not intended to make the teacher uneasy. During the short time the child is with the group, adverse reactions are not at all likely to occur.)

If the teacher has any fears or uncertainties about working with the handicapped child, he or she should discuss these openly with the parents and have them resolved. When effective communication is established, teachers and leaders will find that the child's parents can be their greatest allies.

ASSESSMENT OF THE CHILD'S NEEDS

Before a successful program can be planned to include a handicapped child, two important steps must be taken. First, the leader must decide what the group as a whole should accomplish. Overall goals or guidelines should be recognized, such as understanding the use of symbolism in worship, tracing important events in the life of Christ, learning group camping skills. General goals can then be broken down into specific topics, stories, or skills to be taught over several group sessions. While each leader will eventually develop his or her own set of goals, one suggestion for the novice Christian education teacher (and for parents) is a set of guidelines "for sharing our faith with our children from birth through childhood" written by John H. Westerhoff III: "We need to tell and retell the biblical story — the stories of the faith — together." He mentions, as additional guidelines, that "we need to celebrate our faith and our lives. We need to pray together. We need to listen and talk to each other. We need to perform faithful acts of service and witness together." (Westerhoff, 1980). Goals or guidelines of this nature can be reached by a variety of activities suited to any age level. Most activities can be adapted to include handicapped as well as normal children.

The second step which must be taken is to determine the needs of the handicapped child in reference to the goals and activities planned for the group.

The handicapped child's needs will vary according to the program activities planned. If the activities require the children in the group to read, it will be helpful for the teacher to know whether the handicapped child can read as well as other members of the group. If the stories will be read to the child, the ability to pay attention and listen is needed, a skill which many hyperactive children lack.

Arts and crafts activities require eye-hand coordination, a potential problem area for some learning-disabled and physically handicapped children. Physical strength and coordination are needed for games, dancing, and hiking.

Religious education teachers and other community program leaders can scarcely be expected to perform a sophisticated assessment of a child's abilities, using standardized tests as professional educators do. However, the religious education teacher and community group leader have a different purpose in assessment, because it is not their task to teach basic academic or motor skills. It is their job, rather, to make use of what the child already knows and can already do, and to fit those skills into the group program. How *are* leaders to determine what skills the child possesses?

There are some informal assessment procedures which can be followed. First, much helpful information can be obtained concerning the child's strengths and weaknesses, likes and dislikes, by asking the parents. Care must be taken in interpreting parent responses, however, in that parents do have a biased view of their own children. They may report, for example, that their child can read "pretty well" when the child may in fact be reading far below his or her grade level. They may feel that their child loves to perform in front of a group, yet neglect to say that the only group the child has performed for is a living room full of adoring relatives. The same child might very well panic in front of the whole congregation.

That is not to say that parent assessments cannot be trusted. Parents of exceptional children have been made painfully aware of their children's limitations, and are more apt to be realistic than not. Furthermore, no parents want to see their children fail, and parents of exceptional children have winced at too many failures already. They will not knowingly set their children up for more. But, like all parents, they will be subjective in their assessments, so it is best to use their judgments as only one of several measures.

Another possible source for information about the child's needs is the child's regular school teachers. This source must be approached very cautiously, because professional educators are legally and morally obligated *not* to release any confidential information and must have the parents' consent to discuss the child. They may be able to respond, however, to such a question as, "Miriam Meyer is going to be in my Hebrew school class. Can you suggest any teaching methods or activities that I might be able to use with her?" Again, it must be emphasized that professional teachers should be approached only after the child's parents have given their consent.

Probably the most useful source of assessment is the leader's own observation of the child in action. Does the handicapped child interact well with the other children in the group, or is he or she a loner? Perhaps more opportunities to converse, work and play with classmates are indicated. Does the child seem attentive as you read a story? If not, perhaps shorter stories or more pictures would help. Is there one particular task, such as painting, in which the child gets especially absorbed? If so, that is the teacher's cue to plan for it more often.

It is extremely helpful if there is an assistant leader or other interested adult who can also observe. It is difficult to teach and observe at the same time, and a second observer might pick up clues the teacher would miss.

In general, the purpose of assessing the child's needs is to determine what kinds of activities and content will best help the child to be a happy member of the group.

BEHAVIOR MANAGEMENT

If there is one fear common to new religious education teachers and leaders of other children's programs, it is that the children will misbehave and the teacher will lose control of the group. This fear may be magnified if a handicapped child is included in the group, especially if the child is hyperactive, emotionally handicapped, or generally has the reputation for being "wild."

Fortunately for the teacher, there are a number of things that can be done to manage behavior and bring about an orderly group. One of the very first steps which teachers can take is to examine their own attitudes about children's behavior. Do they believe, for example, that a good child is a quiet child, and a good class must be quiet and calm? If so, there are likely to be problems. Many productive learning experiences take place in an atmosphere of chatter and bustle. When children are excited about what they are doing, there is likely to be noise and activity. This comment does not mean that children must be allowed to scream and "run wild," but rather that some degree of noise is to be expected from a productive group.

It may also be helpful for the teacher to bear in mind that there *will* be a bad day occasionally, even for the best of classes and the most experienced of teachers. The teacher may be a bit less discouraged if he or she remembers that the next session will probably be better, and that there are more good days than bad ones.

Another bit of advice for teachers to remember is that one or more children will sometimes disagree with the teacher, and may even be quite outspoken in their disagreement. This disagreement is rarely intended as a personal affront, so the teacher should try not to get upset by it. A calm reaction to disagreement and even to misbehavior will often defuse a potentially unpleasant situation.

Besides examining personal attitudes toward behavior management, what other steps can the teacher take to encourage a pleasant atmosphere and a well-behaved group of children?

First of all, the teacher can set the stage for desirable behavior in several ways, and thereby prevent problem behaviors from occurring. The classroom or meeting place should be made as attractive as possible, with colorful pictures and an uncluttered furniture arrangement. This step may be difficult if the group meets in a school cafeteria or some other place that is used by other groups during the week. Even then, a portable bulletin board may be available, or perhaps pictures could be temporarily attached (with masking tape only) to the walls. As many distractions as possible should be removed from the meeting area before the children arrive.

The teacher should always arrive early and be available to greet the children as they arrive. Most children, and especially any handicapped children, enjoy such personal attention from an adult. As children arrive, they can be put to work adding pictures to the bulletin board, drawing and coloring, playing with clay, or helping to set out materials and arrange the room. Conversation at this time helps to build rapport between teacher and child. Informal activities such as those mentioned give the children something positive to do and help prevent the chaos which can develop if the children are left, unsupervised, to their own devices.

Next, the teacher should have the day's program carefully planned with a variety of activities. If the teacher is disorganized or has not planned, the children become confused and disorderly. The poorly prepared teacher will rapidly discover the truth of the saying "If you don't have a program for the children, they'll have one for you!"

The idea of variety should be emphasized. Alternating prayer, song, story, artwork, and games will keep the children interested and responsive. By preventing boredom, the teacher can forestall a host of potential behavior problems. Also, providing a variety of activities increases the chance that each child will be able to do something that he or she enjoys and does well. Successful, enjoyable experiences go a long way toward maintaining desirable behavior.

Once the program has been planned, the wise teacher will make a list of all the materials—down to the last pencil and paper clip—that are required for each activity. He or she will then gather all the materials in sufficient quantity for the number of children expected. He or she will group the materials according to activity so that they are readily available when needed during the program. Then the teacher will not have to fumble for them and risk losing the children's attention, thus giving them an opportunity to become rowdy.

If the children are to share materials, such as scissors and glue, the teacher should explain the method for sharing and watch carefully to make sure that every child does get a turn. Good advice to follow in planning any activity, especially a craft project, is for the teacher to do it first. A project which appears on the surface to be very simple may have hidden pitfalls, or it may take longer to do than had been imagined. It is best to know in advance if there are any problems; otherwise, chaos may result when an entire group encounter problems at the same time! Also, special attention can be given to any difficulties which the handicapped child may encounter, and plans to overcome the difficulty can be made in advance.

When the lesson includes a story, especially one from the scriptures, it is best to tell the story rather than read it to the children. Good storytelling takes practice, but the results are well worth the effort. Advantages over reading are many. The teacher can make eye contact with the children, which increases the likelihood of keeping their attention. The style of language in telling a story is more natural than that used in the written version. Greater vocal expression is possible, and it is easier to involve the audience. One technique that works especially well in creating audience involvement is the judicious pause. For example, "And then (pause), what do you suppose happened next? He opened the

door slowly, and there (pause), there on the doorstep he saw (pause)...
the king himself!" The pause creates an eagerness to hear what
comes next.

Pictures to illustrate the story can be very helpful, especially if
they depict costumes, objects, or customs that are very different from
those already known to the child. Pictures also present a concrete
representation, and most children do need concrete images to help
them understand. One caution is offered in regard to the use of pictures.
Children who are mentally retarded and some who are learning-
disabled may be very confused by modern art and symbolism. It is best
to use realistic pictures for these children, because confusion will invite
inattention, "smart aleck" comments, and other undesired behaviors.
Flannelboard figures are another helpful aid for storytelling, and are
readily available at religious bookstores.

When presenting any new project, whether it be a song, a game,
or a craft, it is unwise for the teacher to ask, "Do you want to learn a new
(song, game, etc.)?" Some of the children are almost certain to say no,
and the teacher must then cope with possible dissension and undesirable behavior. It is best simply to announce, "Now we are going to sing a
new song. Here's how it goes," with the confident expectation that
everyone will participate. Usually they will, and those who won't take
part tend to be quiet about it.

Another important aspect of incorporating behavior management
into a well-planned program is to have a ritual beginning and ending to
every meeting. Ritual gives order to the proceedings and gives the
children important cues for how to behave. For example, if the religious
education session always begins with lighting a candle and saying a
prayer, then the act of lighting the candle becomes a cue for the class to
get quiet and pay attention. The program has officially begun. Similarly,
a scout meeting may begin with a flag ceremony. The meeting may end
with a familiar song, with another prayer, a friendship circle, or any
other ritual of the group's choosing. It signals that the meeting is over.
Children need and respond to such cues, so it is important that the ritual
beginning and ending should always be used.

It will be helpful to most teachers to have complete plans written
down for each session. A sample lesson plan is shown in Figure 1.

Two final comments about planning: first, it is usually a profitable
idea to involve the children in the planning process. Children often
make good suggestions for activities they like to do—perhaps for some
that have not occurred to the teacher. When children help with the
planning, they have an investment in the program and will be more

likely to cooperate. Second, it is a good idea to overplan rather than underplan. It is better to have planned more activities than the class can do, than to plan too little and be stuck with extra time during which the class can get rowdy.

Objective	Activity	Materials	Procedure	Evaluation
To help children understand that Jesus helped and healed others	Story of Jesus raising Jarius' daughter	Flannelboard Flannelboard figures in order	Set up background. Add figures as mentioned in story. Remove figures—let children who want to retell story.	Children listened well. Cathy told about her aunt's funeral and seemed upset about it— maybe I should ask her mother about this. *Everybody* wanted to retell the story!
	Mural of Jesus' healing miracles	Picture book for ideas. Mural paper, tape, paints, smocks, brushes, water cans	Divide into groups of 3. Put Charles with Vonnell and Jenny. Each group decide on story to illustrate. Decide who will paint what.	Kids very enthusiastic. Didn't finish— will finish next week. Need more blue paint.

In addition to planning the classroom environment and program, the teachers can also set the stage for good classroom behavior by establishing rules for the group. The children can be involved in making the rules. Rules should be kept brief and to the point. They should also be very specific, because children must know exactly what the teacher wants them to do before they can be expected to do it. Also, the rules should be stated in a positive way. For example, it is better to say "Stay in your seat during story time," than "Don't run around the room." The reason to be positive is twofold. First, the negative statement doesn't tell the child what *to* do; and second, it may give him or her ideas for misbehavior not previously considered!

Following the steps just presented—planning the appearance of the room, planning a good program, and setting up specific rules—should ensure a reasonably well-behaved group. However, even with the best of planning, undesirable behaviors will occur. As long as the misbehaving child is not physically hurting anyone, it is best to ignore—really, systematically ignore — the behavior. When a behavior is first ignored, it will increase for a short time. But if it continues to be ignored, it will cease (be extinguished). Usually it will cease even sooner if the teacher praises desirable behavior while ignoring the unwanted behaviors.

While it is a temptation to punish a child who is misbehaving (usually by scolding), the wise teacher will try to avoid the use of punishment except as a last resort. Punishment does not teach the child what *to* do: it does not produce a desirable behavior. It is more productive to emphasize the desired behavior by letting the children know what they *should* be doing (e.g., "Let's all keep our hands in our laps") rather than what they should *not* be doing ("Let's stop that hitting right now!").

Punishment also produces bad feelings toward the person who does the punishing. The child who is punished may try to avoid the teacher in the future by not coming back to class. Also, the rest of the class may feel uneasy if they see one of their members being punished. The children may then be quiet, but will probably lose their enthusiasm for the activity.

Another problem with punishment is that if the teacher uses it, the children will assume that it is all right for them to use it, too. The teacher serves as a model for the class, and in this case the model would be one for aggression.

One group of researchers (O'Leary, Kaufman, Kass, and Drabman, 1970) has shown that loud reprimands can actually be reinforcing to the child, who thereby receives recognition from the teacher and sympathy from peers. Soft reprimands which are given privately and can be heard only by the child are much more effective. Whenever a reprimand seems necessary, the teacher should remember to give it to the individual student in a soft, calm, matter-of-fact tone of voice. Sarcasm should always be avoided (young children don't understand it anyway), as should personal attacks on the child. A brief comment will be better accepted by the child than will a long sermon. Past misbehaviors should not be brought up for further review; only the present offending behavior should be subject to reprimand. The teacher will do best simply to state what is wrong and what should be done about it.

If a child's misbehavior is so severe that he or she is hurting another member of the group, the teacher will have to remove the child from the group until the misbehavior stops. In such cases (which are fortunately rare), the teacher should discuss the problem with the child's parents and seek their advice and assistance.

If one child is a frequent problem to the teacher, an assistant teacher or aide who could take that child aside for individual activity would be an invaluable help.

A very small number of children are unable to work in a group and must be taught on a one-to-one basis. Such students may display any of a number of unusual behaviors. Long and Frye (1977) list ten behaviors which those students may display:

1. Appear to be "out of contact." The student may be zombie-like in appearance or may be engrossed in a fantasy world.

2. Irrelevant or bizarre talk. A rare student may be echolalic. Or speech may be infantile.

3. Apparent aversion to people. The student may withdraw, isolate himself or herself, and fail to communicate with others.

4. Self-mutilation. For example, the student may continually pick and scratch at herself until she bleeds.

5. Continual rocking, finger wiggling, and extreme fascination with spinning objects.

6. Perseverative behavior, where the student exhibits the same behaviors over and over again.

7. Extremely aggressive or violent behavior.

8. Antisocial behavior, such as lying or stealing.

9. Inability to concentrate or to remain still for more than a few seconds at a time.

10. Excessively fearful or suspicious behavior.

If the teacher notices any of these behaviors, the teacher should discuss the problem with the child's parents and minister or rabbi. Most likely the child's behavior has already been noticed in the school setting, and the child has already been referred for (or may be receiving) special services. The child's parents may be able to suggest methods for helping the child. In any case, the religious education teacher should be aware of the child's need for professional help, and should not try to work with the problem alone.

Severe behavior problems are rare, so the teacher who is uneasy about behavior management should keep in mind that he/she will probably not have to deal with one. In the vast majority of situations, following the behavior management suggestions already presented will result in a well-behaved class that is fun for the children and a pleasure to teach.

GROUP WORK

The group is the fundamental unit for working with children in religious school and community settings. The major purpose for coming to a religious education program, or the scouts and other organizations is to be a member of a group—to enjoy the companionship of others and to strive cooperatively to achieve a common goal. The importance of the group is underscored in Westerhoff's guidelines for sharing our faith with our children. Each one emphasizes the concept of togetherness.

Certainly it is possible to learn by oneself and to perform many activities alone. One can read alone and pray alone. Boy Scouts of America makes provision for the lone scout—a boy who lives in an area so isolated from others that there is no troop available. But the crucial element of sharing, of coming together for a common purpose, is lacking.

Returning to Westerhoff's guidelines, it takes more than one person to tell and retell a story—one to speak and one or more to listen and respond. One cannot celebrate alone; the very essence of the term celebration implies sharing joy with others. While it is possible to pray alone, Jesus himself emphasized the practice of togetherness in prayer when he said, "For where two or three come together in my name, there am I with them" (Matthew 18:20). It clearly requires two or more people to listen and talk to each other. Acts of service require at least one performer and one recipient; witness requires a listener as well as a speaker. Thus, these essential guidelines emphasize the need for working in a group.

For handicapped children, admission to the group has frequently been difficult if not impossible. There were often actual physical barriers to keep handicapped persons out of classes and organizations. Public Law 94-142 has changed the lives of many handicapped children by removing barriers and requiring their inclusion in public education. Mainstreaming has spilled over into other settings as well, so that more and more handicapped children are becoming part of community and religious groups.

In order for each handicapped child to participate fully as a group member, it may be necessary to make some provision for adapting the activity to his or her special needs, or to provide the child with a special helper for part of the session. This does not mean that every lesson must be limited to activities which the handicapped members can easily do! The deaf child may need to see many pictures and may need someone to direct her visual attention, but her presence in the class should not mean that no stories will be told. A physically handicapped scout is not excused from doing the requirements to earn a badge; he can do a ten-mile hike in his wheelchair. What counts most is that the child can participate as a member of the group.

Peer tutors—other members of the class or group—can be especially helpful to a handicapped child who encounters difficulty with an activity, and then both children will enjoy the companionship which giving and receiving such help provides. Cooperative effort is a basic value which all religious education classes and youth groups share, and peer tutoring provides a unique opportunity to put this value into practice.

Special emphasis should be placed on celebrations within the group. The importance of celebration in the church school has been explained by Westerhoff:

Through celebration we find insight for tomorrow. When we share our celebrations with our children, our faith and lives are being shaped together.

That shouldn't be difficult for us to understand. We all love birthday parties and Thanksgiving family meals, Fourth of July picnics, anniversary celebrations, and holiday festivities. Who among us does not like to dress up, decorate, parade, sing, dance, exchange gifts, and eat? Consider the celebration of baptism days, the Eucharist as a family meal, the Pentecost picnic, the anniversary day celebration of saints, and holy day festivities. What are these celebrations without children? To accept children and thus to cater to our own childlike natures is to widen access for ourselves and our children to the world of God.

Some crucial questions we adults need to address are these: What occasions are we going to make special? How will we prepare? What will we do? What part of the story will we remember? What part of our story will we enact? How will we involve children? Only when ritual celebrations become central to the experience we share with our children will Christian faith come to life for us or for them. (pp.45–46)

To handicapped children who have been frequently excluded from celebrations, inclusion in the celebrating group is crucial for their development not only in their faith, but in their understanding of the ideals of any worthwhile group.

CONCLUSION

Teaching any group of children can be an extremely rewarding experience. It can be especially so when a handicapped child has become a full-fledged member of the group. The lives of everyone involved will be enriched. Everyone can gain a new perspective on what it means to be human.

Westerhoff has summed up this perspective in the following comment:

> The norm for human life should not be the physically attractive and capable adult, not the mentally bright, rational adult, not the emotionally stable adult. We would understand human life better if the norm were the exceptional physically, emotionally, mentally retarded child. When we begin our understanding of human life with the fully functioning adult we strive to manipulate the normal child to be like us, and we depreciate and patronize the "abnormal" child because he or she can never be like us. We need to affirm that we are all exceptional children and that they represent what it means to be human. In that important sense true maturity is being what we are to the fullest. If we have been blessed with other physical, emotional, mental, or behavioral gifts, then more will be expected of us, but we will not be of any greater value. Indeed, only as we remember, we capture, and live out the exceptional child in ourselves will we be fully human. (pp. 27–28)

Perhaps that is the ultimate principle upon which religious education should be based.

REFERENCES

Long, J. D. and Frye, V. H. *Making It Till Friday: A Guide to Successful Classroom Management*. Princeton: Princeton Book Company, 1977.

O'Leary, K. D., Kaufman, K. F., Kass, R., and Drabman, R. "The Effects of Loud and Soft Reprimands on the Behavior of Disruptive Students." *Exceptional Children* 37(1970):145–55.
Westerhoff, John H. III. *Bringing Up Children in the Christian Faith*. Minneapolis: Winston Press, 1980.

5

Programming to Meet the Needs of Handicapped Children

Curriculum and Environmental Adaptations

Patricia B. Porter and Grace P. Lane

THE PURPOSE of any religious education or community-based program is to promote congenial social interaction while providing its participants with specific information. Depending upon the program, the information may pertain to religious beliefs and rituals, or perhaps to camping and athletic skills. Whatever the specific focus of the program may be, the leader will undoubtedly want to provide a worthwhile experience for all the members of the group, including the handicapped child. The purpose of this chapter is to help the religious education teacher or youth group leader to adapt the program to accommodate a variety of handicapping conditions.

One basic assumption underlying this chapter is that any handicapped child in the group has already been identified as exceptional by the child's school, physician, or therapist. The religious education teacher, for example, should not be expected to identify or diagnose handicapping conditions.

A second assumption in this chapter is that there are a number of general guidelines which apply to all exceptional children, regardless of the nature of the handicap. These general guidelines will be presented first, followed by specific suggestions for working successfully with a number of handicapping conditions.

GENERAL GUIDELINES

1. The religious education or community-based program is not academic in nature. It is not the religious education teacher's job to

81

dwell upon academic skills. In fact, an academic approach may turn the child off to the program.

It is true that the teacher needs to present some specific content, since that content, be it religious stories, camping skills, or basketball strategy, is the glue which holds the program together and gives it a purpose for existing. It is wise to present the content in a manner which does not expose the child's weaknesses and failings. For example, it would be better for the teacher to tell a story rather than to ask a child with poor reading skills to read it aloud.

Given that disabilities may involve a wide range of activities—reading, speaking, singing, writing, drawing, acting, and dancing (to name a few)—how can the teacher avoid all the activities which create problems for handicapped children and still have a program? The answer is twofold. First, provide for a variety of activities during the year. Provide opportunities for several modes of expression—for verbal response, role-play, arts and crafts, dramatic play, music, outdoor activities, and films. Surely some of the activities will be appropriate for each child. Second, while providing opportunities, don't insist on the child's engaging in any one particular activity. Active involvement in the program is to be encouraged, but the leader should remember that the child may be content sometimes to sit and watch and listen.

2. Don't ignore the handicapped child (or any other child), no matter how baffling or disconcerting his or her problem may be. Some people tend to ignore handicapped people because they don't know how to approach or respond to them. They are afraid of saying the wrong thing and offending the handicapped individual. The teacher can overcome this fear by making a point of greeting each child and asking some informal, conversational question at each session.

3. For achievement-oriented programs such as scouting and Camp Fire Girls, make it possible for the handicapped member to earn the badges, beads, and ranks. Most handicapped children already know that they will have to work longer and harder than other children to accomplish an objective. Like other children, they are proud of genuine accomplishment and are not fooled if an award is handed out automatically.

It may be possible to adapt award requirements for handicapped children by breaking the required tasks down into small steps and letting the child complete one step at a time. The child should be praised for each step completed, and it may be possible to reward him or her at each step with a small, unofficial award such as an attractive sticker or certificate.

The leader should insist upon the child's best effort. If the leader has any questions about the child's ability to perform a given task, he or she should consult the child's parents. The child must not learn to use the handicap as an excuse to circumvent appropriate tasks.

In some religious education programs, awards are given for such activities as memorizing scriptural passages. The teacher should make it possible for the handicapped class member to compete and to earn an award. The child could be given shorter verses to memorize, or perhaps the children could work as partners.

4. It is important that the teacher not pity the handicapped child. The child must learn to cope with his or her disability, and to achieve in spite of it. The teacher should focus on the child's strengths, and build upon what the child *can* do. Thus handicapped children can learn to view themselves as competent persons.

5. For all of the children in the group, the teacher should make liberal use of praise, especially for improvement. Praise strengthens the behavior or activity for which it is given. If the handicapped child cannot yet perform a task as well as the other children in the group, he or she should be praised for any improvement, however small. Thus the child can receive a share of honest praise, and through successive improvements will be able to accomplish the desired task.

The preceding guidelines apply to all handicapped children. The remainder of this chapter will consider further guidelines and modifications which can be used to accommodate specific handicapping conditions. Two types of adaptations will be discussed—curriculum adaptations and environmental adaptations. While it would not be possible to include all possible adaptations for all handicaps, every effort has been made to include those which will be of the greatest benefit to the religious education teacher and community-based group leader.

THE MILDLY MENTALLY RETARDED CHILD

The child who is mildly retarded is very likely to have been mainstreamed into a regular public school class with normal children and probably already knows some of the other members of the church school class. Mildly retarded children usually are no different in appearance from normal children. As long as they are not asked to demonstrate academic skills, they will probably have little if any difficulty in fitting in with the group. They respond well to frequent praise.

Curriculum Adaptations

1. Do arrange activities into small sequential steps and have the child complete one step at a time. He or she may need individual assistance from a teacher, aide, or classmate.

2. These children should not be required to read or write, but they also shouldn't be discouraged from trying if they want to.

3. Use simple vocabulary and explain the meaning of unfamiliar words, or concepts which the child may not understand (e.g., "miracle").

4. Use many pictures or props to illustrate stories, concepts, and terms which may be new to the child, such as *exodus* or *manger*.

5. Use realistic pictures rather than modern art whenever possible. Whereas many normal children enjoy modern art, it may confuse the retarded child.

6. Check the child's memory and understanding of the sequence in a story. Ask if he or she can remember what happened first, what the main character did next, etc. Allow classmates to help.

7. Flannelboard stories are very helpful to retarded children, because they present the story in sequence, add and remove figures at appropriate times, and present children with exactly what they need to see at the moment. Children enjoy retelling a story with flannelboard figures, which serves as a review and as a pleasant, informal test of the child's ability to recall the story.

8. Many religious and community organizations occasionally revise their prayerbooks, hymnals, handbooks, etc., in order to update the language. Some churches use a modern-language version of the Lord's Prayer, some use the traditional King James wording, and some switch back and forth between the different wordings. Scout promises, oaths and laws are occasionally reworded. Retarded children are confused by such changes! Once the retarded child has memorized a set of words, he or she can relearn them or switch to another version only with considerable difficulty, and is likely to regard the new wording as "wrong." The organization as a whole, not just the teacher, should be aware of this problem.

9. Do not expect the retarded child to understand symbolism, except for the most obvious symbols. The understanding of symbolism requires a level of abstract thought seldom attained by retarded children.

Environmental Adaptations

1. Invite the child to sit near you or near an aide or helpful peer. Retarded children may have shorter than average attention spans, and sitting with someone who can keep their attention focused on the lesson may help overcome this problem. Also, the retarded child may have difficulty manipulating scissors and other materials, and may need to be next to someone who can help.

2. Avoid distractions in the classroom or meeting area. Cover up or put away anything you don't want the child to give his or her attention to.

If the meeting room is full of old props or materials (i.e., "junk") from a bygone era, ask to have the stuff removed. If all else fails, it may be advisable to seek a new meeting place. The teacher should never feel hesitant or apologetic about such changes. The environment has a definite influence upon the effectiveness of teaching. Adults who have volunteered their time and energy to work with children deserve to work in an environment which will not sabotage their efforts.

3. During the course of a lesson, bring out visual aids and other materials as they are needed. If they are visible in advance, they may serve as a distraction.

THE LEARNING-DISABLED CHILD

Learning-disabled children are no different in appearance from their normal peers. They have at least average intelligence, and may even be gifted. Learning-disabled children are usually good in some skills and not in others. Any two learning-disabled children are likely to differ greatly in what they do well. One may have difficulty in reading but excel in art; another may read well but be poorly coordinated. Generalizations about learning-disabled students are difficult to make, but frequently they are accused of being lazy by people who are not aware of the learning disability. Because the child can do some things well, they assume that the child is being lazy in the areas of failure. Such is not the case, and the teacher must be patient with the child when he or she is experiencing difficulty in completing some task.

Curriculum Adaptations

1. Don't insist that the learning-disabled child read or write. These skills may be areas of difficulty for the child, and may turn the child off to the program.

2. Artwork and craft projects may be messy in appearance because of the child's lack of eye/hand coordination. Be ready to assist if the child has difficulty in assembling a project.

3. It is essential that the lesson be carefully planned and accurately sequenced. Difficulty in arranging events in correct sequence is a frequent characteristic of learning-disabled children.

4. Learning-disabled children often need to be given very detailed instructions. If a child seems to be having difficulty in completing a project, or even in getting started on a project, he or she may need additional instructions. It is a good idea to have the child repeat the instructions back to you. Such verbalizations help to fix the sequence in the child's mind.

5. Make sure that the child gets the "big picture"—the main idea of the lesson. Many a learning-disabled history student can tell the names of the generals, the detailed battle plans, and the number of casualties on each side—but cannot say who won the war or why it was fought!

6. Many learning-disabled children have a poor sense of time, which includes difficulty in understanding the past. In teaching stories from the scriptures or from centuries past, it will help the child to get a feel for the story if the teacher can "immerse" the class in the story's time period. If possible, talk about and show concrete examples of costumes, food, music, tools, coins, and other cultural artifacts of the time. Ask the children to imagine how the people in the story would have traveled, prepared their food, and performed other acts in their daily lives.

Environmental Adaptations

1. The meeting room should be bright and cheerful in appearance, but not overdone. Too many pictures, props, toys, etc., tend to confuse many learning-disabled students, if these items are displayed all at once. It is best to keep all but a picture or two out of sight until needed in the lesson.

2. Noise may be confusing. Some learning-disabled children are unable to filter out relevant sounds from background noise (even if the

noise is music to everyone else). Even the sound of someone flipping pages in a book can distract some learning-disabled students.

3. Maintain eye contact with the learning-disabled child as much as possible, and encourage the child to maintain eye contact with you. Failure to maintain eye contact is a characteristic of many learning-disabled students, a characteristic which adults tend to find annoying. It gives the impression that the child doesn't care and is not paying attention.

4. If the child is hyperactive (seems to have an attention span of near zero and seems to be everywhere in the room at once), keep him or her close to you. Physical contact, such as an arm around the child's shoulder, often helps increase the child's attention span. Telling the child to "look" at a picture or to "listen" to a statement may help. An aide is an invaluable help. Keep in mind that it is not always a necessity in working effectively with a hyperactive child to keep his or her attention focused on the task at hand.

THE CHILD WITH BEHAVIORAL AND EMOTIONAL PROBLEMS

Children who have been identified as having behavioral or emotional problems represent a wide range of characteristic behaviors. It is difficult to generalize about these children, because their behaviors do vary greatly and may seem to be unpredictable. Some are withdrawn and do not interact with their peers and may not interact with teachers and other adults. They may cry for no apparent reason. Some are said to be "acting-out"; these children tend to exhibit aggressive behaviors such as hitting and cursing when angry. Still others, referred to as "passive-aggressive," are not openly aggressive, but may act out their anger and frustration by ignoring requests, by agreeing to cooperate and then not following through on the promise, or by seeming to misunderstand or not to have heard instructions.

Most children with emotional problems have difficulty making friends. They are not likely to be part of a friendly, supportive group in school or in the neighborhood.

Fortunately for the religious education teacher or scout leader, the child is not likely to cause major problems during the short meeting time, especially if his or her needs are taken into consideration.

Three notes of caution are in order. First, children with behavioral and emotional problems are not "crazy." They do not tend to exhibit bizarre behaviors, and they do not tend to be out of touch with reality. They exhibit the same behaviors as normal children, but they do so to excess. Most normal children do occasionally scream, curse, hit, kick, taunt, cry, and ignore. Emotionally handicapped children do these same things much more frequently.

Second, since normal children do display these undesirable behaviors, the religious education teacher is cautioned against assuming or fearing that all children who do these things are emotionally handicapped. Otherwise there will be days when the teacher may suspect that the entire class has emotional problems!

Third, the religious education teacher or community-based group leader who has an identified emotionally handicapped child in the group should not try to be a therapist. Only a professional counselor, psychologist, or psychiatrist should assume that role.

It should also be noted that many children with emotional problems also have learning disabilities, so all of the adaptations suggested for the learning disabled child can be applied to this child as well.

Curriculum Adaptations

1. Many emotionally handicapped children enoy and do well with art projects. They need to be *actively involved* in a project. It is wise to include many opportunities for painting, coloring, and drawing.

2. Emotionally handicapped children may learn best in small, closely supervised groups, or on a one-to-one basis with the teacher or aide. It is a good idea to provide individual attention for this child.

3. Music can be a good activity for this child, especially action songs. The *Cub Scout Songbook* is an excellent and inexpensive source of easy-to-sing action songs. Again, active involvement is the key to success for this activity.

4. Ask this child's opinion occasionally. People rarely do, and the child is flattered to be asked—although the opinion expressed may be painfully candid! The emotionally handicapped child can reason as well as his or her normal peers, and may provide the class with surprising insights.

5. Puppets and stuffed animals as media for acting out feelings and situations work wonders with emotionally handicapped children. Even older children—up to and including junior high school—seem to enjoy activities involving their use.

Environmental Adaptations

1. Especially if the child tends to exhibit aggressive behaviors, don't make available any materials that he or she could tamper with and destroy, or could use to injure someone.

CHILDREN WITH COMMUNICATION DISORDERS

All that interaction which we call communication involves essentially three parts: (1) a message sender, (2) a message, and (3) a message receiver. There can occur in children breakdowns in the expression of the message or the reception of the message. In modifying curriculum and environment for children having communication disorders, it is helpful and practical to view their difficulty as it affects "information in" or "information out." The child with a hearing handicap has difficulty receiving the message—information in. A child with a speech difficulty has trouble expressing the message—information out.

Children with language problems, although they may have good hearing and an intact speech mechanism (lips, tongue, teeth, jaw, palate), may have what we call a central disorder. That is, the message can be heard and it can be spoken; the breakdown lies in what happens to that message when it gets past the hearing mechanism and before it reaches the speech mechanism. A language disorder affects the processing of the message that occurs in the brain. Areas of perception, memory, and message planning may all be affected when there is a language disorder.

Speech, language, and/or hearing disorders are often mistakenly associated with low intellectual functioning or mental retardation. While mentally retarded persons can have speech, language, or hearing problems, these communication disorders can occur in children having average or even above average intelligence. Communication affects every aspect of each of our lives. Social interaction, learning, and job achievement are all dependent upon the ability to communicate. Children with communication handicaps often feel isolated by their inability to make others understand them or to understand others. Close observation of the way a child attempts to communicate and reinforcement of successful communication attempts, as well as patience and understanding are essential in working with the child with a communication handicap.

Speech Disorders

There are several kinds of speech disorders that may affect a child's ability to express a message. *Articulation disorders* affect how a child puts speech sounds together to form words. A problem may involve omission of some speech sounds in words, addition of some speech sounds, substitution of one speech sound for another, or distortion of speech sounds. Articulation disorders vary from being mildly distracting to rendering the child totally unintelligible. *Stuttering* is another speech disorder. Stuttering involves the interruption of the flow of speech. Children with this difficulty often repeat sounds in words or prolong sounds. *Voice disorders* affect the tone and volume of the child's speech. These children often sound as if they have a cold or sore throat all the time. There are children who have a *total absence of speech*. This occurs only in connection with another disability such as a physical handicap, mental retardation, or an extreme emotional disturbance. These children are unable to communicate at all using speech.

Language Disorders

Language disorders can affect the way children understand directions and their ability to communicate a reply. These children often have difficulty selecting the right word to express what they want or putting words into the proper sequence to form sentences. Children with language difficulties often have problems with reading, writing, and spelling.

Hearing Disorders

There are varying degrees of hearing loss (see also discussion in Chapter Two). With a mild hearing loss, the child can understand almost everything that is said to him or her, but often misunderstands sounds that are similar and depends a great deal on visual cues to understand speech. On the other hand, the child with a severe hearing loss may not be able to hear any sound and must depend totally on visual cues. Children who have had hearing and then lost it due to illness or injury are better able to understand speech than children who have been hearing-impaired from birth and have never had the opportunity to hear speech. Also, children who have acquired a hearing loss often have better speech themselves, in that they have been able to monitor their own emerging speech. We all depend on our own hearing to monitor and correct our speech production. When children cannot hear themselves speak, it is difficult for them to make appropriate adaptations in their speech. Therefore, the speech of severely hearing impaired children is often distorted and difficult to understand, even though the speech mechanism itself is fine.

Curriculum Adaptations

Articulation Difficulties

1. The child is probably aware of having a speech difficulty and is more than likely working on the problem with a speech therapist. It is not your responsibility to attempt to correct the child's defective speech; in fact, doing so many further draw attention to the speech difficulty and embarrass the child. It is better to attempt to listen to *what* the child is saying rather than *how* he or she is saying it.

2. It will be easier to understand the child's single word productions rather than connected speech. It is a good idea then, to design your questions so that the child will only have to answer using one or two word utterances. For instance: "Joshua, do you want the red paper or the blue?" Rather than "Joshua, what do you want?"

3. It is not unusual for children with articulation problems to vary in their ability to produce clear speech. Encourage the child to talk during the periods in which he or she is most understandable.

4. Allow all talking to be voluntary. Do not force the child to talk if he or she is hesitant to do so, but encourage conversation when you can.

5. Use visual materials whenever possible. Allow the child to point to a picture by way of response if he or she cannot correctly utter the appropriate word.

6. Do not force the child to compete for your attention with the other members of the group. Give your attention when he or she is attempting to communicate. Do not act as if you understand what the child has said if you do not. It is better to respond by saying, "Joshua, I am having some difficulty understanding what you're saying to me, but I am anxious to know what you think. Please tell me again, and I will listen harder this time." Above all, be patient.

Stuttering

1. Most children go through a period of normal nonfluency during their preschool years. These hesitations and prolongations in speech do not constitute stuttering at all. Rather, they reflect that the child may have more to say than he or she has the ability to say it. This normal nonfluency is not accompanied by any struggle or tension on the child's part. The group leader can best attend to this by not attending at all. Do not call attention to the child's difficulties by having him or her "slow down and take a deep breath," or "stop, and start over again." The child will outgrow this speech difficulty if he or she is not made to feel that speech is difficult and that he or she "doesn't do it very well."

2. Children who do, in fact, stutter are certainly most aware of it. It does not help to call further attention to it by offering any of the suggestions listed above. These suggestions do not help, and they often act to frustrate the child further and reinforce the idea that talking is an awful endeavor that ought to be avoided at all costs.

3. Children can often sing, or recite poems or verses, without stuttering at all. Role playing is another activity that can be engaged in without any fluency problems. These would be excellent vehicles to use in allowing the child to participate in a group and to achieve some success.

4. Do not interrupt the child when he or she is speaking. Let the child speak at his or her own rate and be willing to allow the child to stutter.

5. Allow all speech responses to be voluntary, but encourage conversation when possible, especially when the child is relaxed and stuttering is not so severe.

Voice Disorders

1. Ordinarily, no curriculum modifications need to be made for these children. However, the parents or the speech therapist may ask you to have the child refrain from singing or shouting for a period of time.

Total Absence of Speech

1. Visual materials are a necessity here. If the child cannot or will not speak, have him or her respond by pointing to a picture or a sequence of pictures.

2. Many nonverbal children use "communication boards." These children have already learned that the way they must communicate is by pointing to pictures, words, or symbols. The child uses this board as his or her voice, and you can assist by paying attention as if the child were talking to you. It's a very good idea to have the child's parents show you how the child uses the communication board before you attempt to interact with him or her by yourself.

3. Many nonverbal children use manual communication (sign language similar to that used by deaf persons). It would be helpful for the group leader to learn some signs, (perhaps as an activity with other children in the group), especially those used most frequently by the child, so that communication could take place. In some instances, the child may need an interpreter who understands sign language very well to assist you in communicating with the child.

Language Disorders

1. It may be helpful to repeat what the child says (especially if the child has selected the wrong word or if the sentence is out of sequence). In repeating, however, the group leader should say what the child has said correctly and perhaps expand on it a bit. It is easier to teach the child by giving feedback rather than by correcting him or her. This acts to reinforce the child's talking and to make it a pleasurable experience.

2. It is helpful both to talk about what you're doing, and also to talk to the child about what he or she is doing or thinking. The child learns new words and correct sentence production by hearing them first.

3. Talk about what has just happened. This not only helps the child to learn new words and correct sentences, it also allows him or her to get some practice in sequencing events.

4. Use visual materials whenever possible. Name what you see as you point to it.

5. The flannelboard is a valuable teaching tool for the language-disordered child. It allows the child to see the picture of the word you're describing and see how it fits appropriately into a sequence. Stories can even be presented using the flannelboard as a prop. The child can assist by putting the pictures in proper order as the story progresses.

6. Leave out the last word of a sentence and have the child fill it in. If he or she doesn't know the answer, you can help by allowing the child to see a picture of the word that is missing.

7. Avoid abstractions. The child will be more successful if the concepts are concrete and the materials are "seeable" and "touchable."

8. Children with language problems often love rhythm and rhyme. Songs, poems, verses and stories with built-in sound effects are enjoyable.

9. But don't insist that the language-disabled child read or write. These skills may be areas of difficulty for the child who should be allowed to participate in the group in other ways.

Hearing Disorders

1. The child who has a hearing loss needs to develop habits of attention. It will take this child longer to perceive what is being communicated. Allow him or her to watch your facial movement and expression, because the child's eyes and ears must work together.

2. Use visual materials whenever possible, but do not neglect to say the word as you point to the picture. The child must learn to connect the sound, and the lip and facial movements, with the object.

3. Make use of all opportunities to use speech when the child is within hearing distance. Have fun imitating sounds and encourage the child to make noises and sounds as he or she plays.

4. Stimulate listening by providing experiences with items that make noise. Rhythmic activities and dance are often enjoyable for the hearing-impaired child.

5. Do not overwhelm the hearing-impaired child with lots of words. Describe the activity that you are doing in as few words as possible and don't overemphasize the pronunciation of the words or speak very loudly.

6. The hearing-impaired child may use manual communication (sign language). It would be good for the group leader to learn some of the signs that the child frequently uses, perhaps teaching some to other children in the group at the same time. In some situations it may be preferable to enlist the help of an aide who knows sign language and can interpret the child's messages for you.

Environmental Adaptation

1. Invite the communication-handicapped child to sit near you, near an aide or a helpful friend. This will reduce the amount of competition for communication that the child may feel and will allow him or her

to seek ready assistance when he or she cannot understand or cannot make himself or herself understood.

2. Make sure the hearing impaired child is seated so that he or she can readily see the group leader. Make sure that there is no glare on the group leader's face, and that the group leader does not turn away from the child to face the other side of the room, or to face the blackboard when he or she is speaking to the group.

3. The child with a hearing impairment may wear a hearing aid. It is a good idea to ask the parents of the child about the fit of the aid and the proper volume setting. It is also a good idea to have spare hearing aid batteries with you, just in case the child's battery runs out during your time with him or her.

4. Noise will be confusing and distracting to the communication-handicapped child. Especially for the hearing-impaired child, noise in the environment may interfere with the child's ability to hear what you're saying. Try to make the environment as free from distracting noise as possible.

CHILDREN WITH VISUAL HANDICAPS

The term visual handicap is used when a child has a vision problem that affects learning. Visual handicaps directly interfere with the child's ability to gain information through the visual channel, and may interfere with the ability to act on that information in ways such as moving about in the environment. The degree of handicap can range from partial sight to complete blindness. Some children with very little sight can use what they have more effectively than others who have a good deal more visual ability. It is difficult, then, to plan a program based solely on medical information about the child's visual ability. Awareness, understanding, and acceptance of children's visual problems and careful observation of what they do and how they do it are far more helpful to you in planning for them than any definitions based on visual acuity.

Curriculum Adaptations

1. Children with a severe visual handicap may display mannerisms that seem to provide the stimulation they are otherwise deprived of by their lack of vision. Children may rock their bodies, turn

their heads from side to side, flutter fingers in front of their faces, or constantly tap toys or other objects. Often the mannerisms are uncomfortable for others to look at, and they make the child seem "different" to other children. If so, offer the child a substitute activity.

2. Children with visual handicaps sometimes may seem to be unresponsive and to lack curiosity. They sometimes hold their heads down, because they don't need to hold them up to see; or it may be easier for them to hear with their heads bent slightly downward. Being unable to see, they cannot react to others' facial expressions. Therefore they have no need to look into the face of the person with whom they are speaking. This makes them seem uninterested. It is important to keep this in mind and realize that, in presenting information to the visually impaired child, you cannot use appearance as a barometer of level of interest.

3. Let visually handicapped children hold objects as near to their eyes as they wish and at any angle they select. Children discover for themselves how to hold objects at the best angle and distance for seeing.

4. For partially sighted children, use simple, clear, uncluttered illustrations. You can even make the central figures of pictures bolder by outlining them with felt tip pens.

5. Employ the child's sense of hearing, touch, taste and smell in presenting materials. Because the child will not be able to acquire information through the visual channel, he or she will have to depend on the other senses.

6. Your verbal explanations should be clear and direct. Avoid the use of vague designations such as *this, that,* and *over there.*

7. Some blind and visually handicapped children will employ the use of braille (a system of writing which uses raised dots to represent letters). Be sure that important written materials (scout manuals, Bibles, etc.) are available in braille. These, as well as large print books, can be obtained from the American Printing House for the Blind (see resource listing beginning p. 000).

8. The child with a visual handicap cannot observe your preparations for the next activity. Inform him or her of what will happen next so that the child can prepare for a change in the activity.

9. Show your feelings to this child with a hand on the shoulder or arm, or a hug or pat on the head, instead of a smile or the eye-to-eye contact you would give a seeing child.

Environmental Adaptations

1. Encourage the child to move freely to wherever an activity is occurring. Make sure there are no objects in the way to be stumbled over.

2. Visually handicapped children often need to be shown the correct position for sitting and standing. Assist by placing the child physically in the appropriate position for sitting in a circle or standing in line.

3. When the child becomes used to the set-up of the environment, do not unexpectedly change the position of chairs, tables, or other objects, without showing the child the changes that are being made. Avoid changing the position of items in the room if at all possible.

4. Some children can benefit from desks with adjustable tops so that they can move written material closer or farther away as needed.

5. When walking with the visually impaired student, do not take his or her hand and lead. It is better to grasp the child's arm lightly, just above the elbow, and walk about a half step behind in a natural manner. It will be a good idea to instruct other children in the group in how to do this.

CHILDREN WITH ORTHOPEDIC HANDICAPS

Orthopedic handicaps are conditions that primarily limit the child's physical abilities. These handicaps are usually visible either because of the awkward way the child moves, or the devices such as wheelchairs, braces, and artificial limbs that he or she must use in order to move. Children may have orthopedic handicaps as a result of conditions associated with birth defects, accidents, or diseases. Conditions might include, for example, spina bifida, loss or deformity of limbs, burns which cause contractures, or cerebral palsy.

Curriculum Adaptations

1. Learn all you can about the child's specific handicap. Seek out advice from the child's parents about what the child can and cannot do. Learn the child's strengths as well as his or her needs. And learn what

you can reasonably expect from the child in terms of motor activities, so that you will know how much or how little he or she actually needs.

2. Avoid being overprotective, but be alert to the child's needs for support.

3. Use physical contact to help the orthopedically handicapped child. Place your hand on his or her hand to assist with painting or coloring.

Environmental Adaptations

1. The orthopedically handicapped child needs to feel comfortable and well balanced in order to participate in activities. Make sure the child is properly supported and comfortable and has maximum freedom to see what he or she is doing. Parents can be very helpful in assisting you with determining the proper position for various activities.

2. Make sure that the room is free of obstructions, and that there is enough room for the child to move about on crutches, with a walker, or in a wheelchair.

3. Eye level is different for children in wheelchairs, and the reaching ability of children using wheelchairs, crutches, or other devices may be limited. Be sure to adapt activity areas accordingly.

4. Enlist the support of other members of the group to help push the child's wheelchair, or adjust its position. This can be a valuable interaction for the handicapped child and a nonhandicapped friend.

CHILDREN WITH EPISODIC HANDICAPS

There is a group of health problems that may interfere on an episodic basis with the child's ability to learn and to interact. These health problems are often called "invisible handicaps" because the children appear to be perfectly healthy most of the time. With proper ongoing medical care, these children may never need any other sort of special services.

Epilepsy or Convulsive Disorders

In these disorders, there is a sudden temporary excess of energy in the brain, which interrupts normal activity and results in a seizure. This interruption may be as simple as a staring spell only a few seconds long, as in petit mal seizures, or as dramatic as a few minutes of jerking movement, as in grand mal seizures. There are other types of seizures, but these are the most common. During the seizure, the child's normal activity is briefly interrupted and some type of reaction takes its place. Following the seizure, some children sleep for a few minutes to a few hours, and other children seem unaffected. While some mentally retarded children have convulsive disorders as well, most persons with convulsive disorders are *not* mentally retarded. Epilepsy is not related to mental illness. There are many myths and misconceptions about epilepsy, but as we learn more about it, we find that it is, in fact, a neurologic disorder for which, in most children, medication can provide total control or even elimination of the seizures.

Diabetes

Children with diabetes have an inadequate or inefficient supply of insulin in their blood. Children with diabetes need supplements of insulin and are often given shots every day. While these children can lead normal lives, special attention must be given to the kinds of food they eat.

Asthma

Asthma is a condition most usually caused by an allergy to some material. That material varies from child to child. With asthma, there is usually a rather sudden onset of difficulty which involves moving the air in and out of the lungs (especially out of the lungs). In most instances, asthma can be controlled by medication taken orally or in a fine mist that can be inhaled.

Hemophilia

This is a condition that is inherited and affects male children. Children with hemophilia cannot control bleeding once their bodies are cut or bruised. When bleeding does occur, medical treatment is necessary to replace blood lost and supply medicine that helps the blood to clot. If there have been recurrent episodes of bleeding, sometimes the children have deformities in their joints; otherwise, the children appear to be perfectly healthy.

Curriculum Adaptations

1. Curriculum adaptations are not usually necessary for this group of children.

Environmental Adaptations

1. It is important for you to find out all you can about the child's particular disorder. It will help to know how often the child is apt to have an episode of difficulty, and what to do under those circumstances. The parents can be very helpful in supplying this information.

2. Many children with health impairments must receive daily medication to control their condition. It is not likely that you will ever be asked to administer any medication; however, during day-long activities or overnight outings, be sure the proper supply of medication is brought along and administered on time; you yourself should know the exact amount to be given.

3. Seizures are best handled by allowing the child to remain where he or she is when the seizure begins, or by gently lowering the child to the floor. Make sure the child does not get injured during the seizure. Do not try to stop the child's movements, and do not attempt to put anything in the child's mouth. It might be helpful to turn the child's head to one side, so that any material accumulated in the mouth may drain out. If the child has two grand mal seizures, one right after another, this could signal a medical emergency. Be sure to have the child's physician's name close at hand or call an ambulance to take the child to the hospital. This type of emergency happens very rarely. Seizures are not painful and they do not harm a child. Afterward, however, the child may be frightened or a little confused. You may wish to spend some time talking privately with him or her and providing some gentle support and reassurance.

4. Children with hemophilia bleed the same amount as other people; they just don't stop bleeding. For minor cuts, a Band-Aid firmly applied will stop the bleeding. Deep cuts provide more difficulty. For a deep cut, heavy fall, or any head injury, the child with hemophilia will need medical attention. The chances of this happening are very slight.

5. Some children with episodic handicaps may need some restrictions of activities. Activity is ordinarily determined by the child's tolerance and by his or her history of activity-related difficulty. The child's parents can provide guidelines regarding any restrictions necessary.

6. Foster independence. Encourage the child to do the things that he or she can do, and offer praise for jobs well done.

THE SEVERELY MENTALLY RETARDED CHILD

Severely retarded individuals almost always have significant central nervous system damage, and often other handicapping conditions exist as well. Training for the severely retarded person typically consists of self-care skills, such as toileting, dressing, eating, drinking, and language development. Sometimes, the severely retarded person is unable to care for his or her personal needs and may be confined to a bed or wheelchair.

Because of their great physical, mental, and behavioral limitations, severely handicapped children grow, learn, and develop much more slowly than any other group of children. Recent changes in teaching technology have shown, however, that severely retarded persons can learn skills that once were considered beyond their capability. Children with severe handicaps are, first of all, people. They are an extremely heterogeneous group and very diverse in behavior and capabilities. The differences among severely handicapped children are greater than their similarities.

Curriculum Adaptations

1. Severely mentally retarded children benefit greatly from social interaction. Even though you may feel that the child is not learning the information that you are trying to put forth, be assured that the child is gaining much from the stimulation that you are providing and from the presence of the other children.

2. Many severely retarded children have significant communication handicaps. Some of them are totally nonverbal. It would be a good idea, when possible, for you to use the suggestions for adaptation of curriculum listed in the section "Total Absence of Speech" beginning on page 92.

3. These children have specific personality traits just like other children. They have likes and dislikes. It will be helpful for you to learn what activities the child enjoys in order to make use of them in your program. For instance, if the child likes singing, you might use a song to get your message across.

4. In working with the severely retarded child on a particular task, remember that the child needs clear instructions from the group leader before performing the task, and immediate feedback and reinforcement afterwards.

Environmental Adaptations

1. Many of these children will require the use of adaptive equipment, such as wheelchairs, braces, or communication boards. Be sure to find out how these pieces of equipment work before you attempt to interact with the child by yourself. Parnets can be very helpful in providing such information.

2. Arrange the environment so that the severely handicapped child will not be isolated. The child should be able to see you and to see and interact with the other members of the group.

3. Do not force the child to interact if he or she has difficulty in doing so. Remember that the child will benefit by observing the action of the group and by the social interaction the group provides.

CHILDREN WITH DEGENERATIVE DISEASES

Most handicapping conditions are relatively stable. Children with cerebral palsy or mental retardation rarely get worse. There is a group of handicapping conditions, however, that are identified as degenerative or progressive in nature. The child with one of these diseases becomes steadily weaker and more handicapped as time progresses. These children almost always have shortened life spans. It is very important for these children to participate in as many enjoyable group activities as possible. For the child with a disease that has no cure, we must strive to improve the quality of life because, in many instances, we will not be able to act successfully to lengthen the child's life.

Muscular Dystrophy

Muscular dystrophy is the name applied to a group of diseases that are characterized by gradual wasting of the muscle, with accompanying weakness and deformity. Children with muscular dystrophy can begin to have difficulty with muscle control as early as three years of age. They become progressively weaker and eventually must depend on braces, and then wheelchairs, in order to move around in their environment. Children with muscular dystrophy often spend a good deal of time in the hospital undergoing surgical procedures that will allow them to be mobile for as long as possible. There is no medicine that can be given to help or cure muscular dystrophy.

Cystic Fibrosis

This is a condition in which the glands secrete a very sticky substance which produces digestion and breathing problems. The child with cystic fibrosis is usually small in stature and may have a chronic cough and asthma-like breathing. Children with cystic fibrosis can sometimes take medicines that will temporarily relieve their symptoms. They often spend time in the hospital because of frequent episodes of pneumonia and should not be exposed to other children with colds and respiratory problems if at all possible.

Cancer

Cancer is an abnormal growth of cells. It can occur in any part of the body. The causes of cancer are unknown. The most important fact to remember is that cancer, like muscular dystrophy and cystic fibrosis, is not contagious. Today the child with cancer stands a better chance than ever before of surviving and living a normal life. The child may spend time in the hospital due to surgery, radiation therapy, chemotherapy, or combinations of the above therapies. Due to these various therapies, the child with cancer often undergoes visible changes. It is not unusual for the child to experience hair loss, weight gain or loss, or loss of limbs.

Curriculum Adaptations

1. Adaptations will need to be made according to the specific needs of the child. It is important to note that the specific needs of the child may change with time, and, therefore, it is not practical to assume that program planning that was appropriate in September will also be appropriate in January.

2. To facilitate continued participation in the group, it is very helpful if a child can maintain some contact with you during his or her inevitable periods of absence. Home or hospital visits, cards and calls from you or members of the group will be very valuable.

Environmental Adaptations

1. Adaptations will depend upon the specific needs of the child. Again, these may change as the disease progresses.

2. Depending upon the effect of disease, environmental adaptations suggested in the sections on "Children with Orthopedic Handicaps" on page 00 and "Children with Episodic Handicaps," page 00, could apply to these children as well.

Special Considerations

Children with degenerative, life-threatening diseases present some unique problems. As the child becomes more handicapped, he or she may become depressed or withdrawn. The child may begin to feel less and less like a worthwhile person. It will be important for you to know how much the child knows about the illness. Children are usually best able to cope with their illness and treatment if they know as much as possible about it. Therefore, children and their parents are ordinarily told the diagnosis, the means of treatment to be used, and the chances of controlling or curing the disease. This information can be obtained from the child's parents. The other children in the group may ask questions about the child's condition. Ask the parents about their feelings before giving the group members such information. If the parents and the child are willing, it may help to tell the group about the type of disease the child has and the kind of treatment being received. This open approach is particularly useful in dealing with some of the side effects of treatment, such as weight gain or hair loss. Degenerative diseases are particularly difficult for adolescents. At a time when their peers are becoming more independent, the adolescent with a degenerative disease is becoming more dependent. At a time when peer acceptance assumes vital importance, the teenager with a degenerative disease may feel "different," both by the fact of the disease and by the visible manifestations of it. The older child may think more about the effect of the illness on future plans, and is more likely than the younger child to dwell on the possible fatal outcome of the disease. The group leader can provide special support to the child and his or her family by allowing them to speak openly about the disease. The child's sense of self-approval and general outlook on life is greatly influenced by other people. The group leader can influence the child and the rest of the group by conveying that you like the child and that you are glad that he or she is there.

CHILDREN WITH MULTIPLE HANDICAPS

Multiply handicapped children have combinations of obvious and sometimes not so obvious disabilities. It is not unusual for the severely retarded child also to have physical handicaps such as difficulty with muscles, possibly speech and language problems, perhaps an emotional disability, or visual or auditory problems. Some children have combined deafness and blindness. It is often difficult to ascertain the exact nature and extent of the child's multiple handicaps. These children are often so seriously handicapped that they certainly need very special equipment and services.

Curriculum Modifications

1. Multihandicapped children need highly individualized treatment. Attention needs to be paid to the type and degree of the child's handicap. For instance, if a child is partially deaf and has no vision at all, your interaction with the child will make use of the hearing that he or she does have. It is vitally important to know not only the weaknesses that these children have, but also their strengths, because their strengths are what you will use to teach and interact with them.

2. These children have specific personalities and likes and dislikes just as other children do. It is a good idea to identify the things and the activities that the child likes, so that you may employ them to make the child's participation in your group as enjoyable as possible.

3. Depending upon the type and degree of handicaps that the child presents, suggestions made in the sections on mentally retarded, communication handicapped or visually impaired children will be appropriate.

4. Invite the child to participate in group activities at his or her level. Remember that the child can benefit from observing the other members of the group and socially interacting with them and with you.

5. Allow the child to be as independent as possible. Design activities so that the child will be successful using the skills that he or she has. The partially deaf, blind child, for instance, can enjoy working with clay, swaying to music, and exploring objects by touch. Provide physical assistance when necessary and encourage the other members of the group to do the same.

Environmental Adaptations

1. Multihandicapped children often need special equipment, such as wheelchairs, hearing aids, or communication boards. Be sure to become familiar with these devices before you attempt to interact with the child by yourself. Parents can be very helpful in orienting you to the design and use of these devices.

2. Arrange the classroom so that the child can be independent and as mobile as possible, and do not make unexpected changes. Keep adaptive equipment near the child so that he or she may have access to it as needed.

3. Allow the multiply handicapped child to sit near you or near a helpful friend. In this way, the child can request assistance easily when it is needed.

The most important point to remember in adapting curricula and environment for any handicapped child is that each child is an individual. Whether deaf, blind, or retarded, handicapped children are first and foremost people. Your task will be to see the handicap, learn about it, and devise the methods to work through it to meet the child to whom the handicapping condition belongs.

⑥
The Community
Its Services and Service Providers

Bobbie B. Lubker

THIS CHAPTER DISCUSSES exceptional individuals and their families in the community, and the services and support which exist beyond the family. Many communities have a rich variety of professional people and agencies serving exceptional individuals of all ages. In obtaining help for exceptional populations, it is important to learn what is already available, to assist families in attaining access to existing services, and to develop services appropriate for the community and its citizens.

Individuals who are active in religious and other organizations may take their own children to private pediatricians, dentists, speech clinicians, or psychologists. However, a large proportion of individuals with special needs are eligible for services provided through public systems and through volunteer or social agencies. Those unfamiliar with these resources, may find it worthwhile to investigate what services are available and how people may qualify for them. For instance, how do people get food stamps? How can a child get surgery for a cleft palate? Where can a child get a hearing aid? Who provides wheelchairs? What agencies provide help for adults?

COMMUNITY RESOURCES: PUBLIC AGENCIES

1. *Local and State Health Departments* provide preventive health programs and services which encourage and promote personal and community health. These include:

Clinical Services

Chronic disease screening and monitoring
Dental care for children and adults
Eye examinations
Family planning
Immunization services (some immunizations are required by law
   before children may be admitted to school)
Maternity care, including prenatal counseling
Pediatric services, including well-child clinics
Venereal disease prevention

Community Services

Communicable disease reporting
Community nursing
Environmental health services (standards in food handling, lodg-
   ing, water supplies, and waste disposal are monitored)
Health education services
School health services
Registration of births and deaths
Disease surveillance

2. *State Crippled Children's Services* are designed to provide
health care for individuals under twenty-one who have conditions
which may hinder normal growth and development. Multi-disciplinary
health care is provided using the skills of several health professionals.
Financial assistance is available for eligible patients. Clinics may exist
for orthopedic or speech and hearing problems, for congenital and
rheumatic heart disease, for neurologic and seizure disorders, for cleft
lip–cleft palate, cystic fibrosis, and kidney disease. Eligibility is determined in most states by the Crippled Children's Program of the Division
of Health Services; decisions are based on age, residence, and medical
condition and on family resources. Application can be made through
local health departments, hospitals, physicians, nursing, or social work
consultants. Information is available through the national offices of the
Bureau of Community Health Services (Crippled Children's Services,
Family Planning Services, Office for Maternal and Child Health), 5600
Fishers Lane, Rockville, Maryland 20850.

3. *The Department of Social Services* is funded by county, state, and federal governments and provides financial and social services to the community.

Financial services include Aid to Families with Dependent Children (AFDC), general assistance, Medicaid, food stamps, and Title XX certification (federally funded services such as day care, chore services, and protective services).

Family and children's services include maternity home placements, adoption services, foster care services, institutional placement referrals, homemaker services, psychological testing and consulting, protective services (child abuse and neglect), day care, family casework, paternity and support, and family planning.

Adult services may include licensing and supervision of rest homes, nursing home placements, homemaker services, casework services, family planning, protective services, and chore services.

Referral to other programs and services may be made to vocational rehabilitation programs, state commissions for the blind, programs to meet the needs of alcoholics or drug abusers, and other agencies.

4. *The State Department of Public Instruction (SDPI), Division of Exceptional Children* is the coordinating agency for education of all exceptional children in public schools. It develops guidelines for determining child classifications and program needs, and provides consultants to local schools to develop services. Statistical data, legal issues, education trends, teacher education standards, and other considerations are the responsibility of SDPIs in each state. They also furnish information on school services for exceptional children in all school systems.

5. *State Division of Services for the Blind* secures services to overcome the handicapping effects of blindness, and to improve the individual's functioning in daily living and working. Services may include casework, group work and community services; educational and recreational services; provision of special equipment and transportation assistance; and mobility training and self-help skills. This agency maintains a register of legally blind people; individuals with specified levels of visual impairment are eligible for services. Representatives may usually be contacted through county or city departments of social services or through health departments.

6. *Other state departments.* Most states have other administrative units which provide consultation and service for disabled populations. Administrative units with titles like "Department of Human Resources" employ professionals whose primary mission is to serve exceptional children and adults.

7. *Mental Health Clinics*. There are approximately two thousand mental health clinics in the United States; they are usually operated by mental health centers (see below), hospitals, and other agencies, although about four hundred are under private auspices (Goldenson, 1978).

8. *Community Mental Health Centers*. The Mental Health Centers Act of 1963 provided for the development of coordinated mental health services to provide treatment in home communities. In the late 1970s, funding for more than three hundred centers in the United States came from federal, state, and county tax dollars and client fees. Programs and specific services vary from one center to another. Variability is related to factors such as community needs in rural, suburban or urban areas, personnel qualifications, and community commitment to mental health services. Centers provide mental health information and training to citizens. Most centers do not offer all of the program examples listed below; however, each of the services is provided in one center or another in the mental health center network:

Outpatient therapy for children, adults, and families
In-patient treatment for emergency cases or chronic cases
Twenty-four-hour emergency phone systems and "help lines"
Partial hospitalization on a day, night, or weekend basis for children and adults
Rehabilitation for patients and former patients
Precare before hospitalization and aftercare following hospitalization
Special programs for alcoholics, drug addicts, abused children
Transitional living facilities
Consultation to physicians, clergy, health departments, schools, courts, and police
Training for personnel
Research and evaluation of programs (Goldenson 1978)

Some special services under the umbrella of a mental health center are offered in some communities:

Special child evaluation and treatment
Workshops for handicapped adults
Group homes for children and adults
Preschools for handicapped children

COMMUNITY RESOURCES: ORGANIZATIONS, ASSOCIATIONS, AND AGENCIES

Scores of professional associations, advocacy groups, and volunteer organizations exist in the United States with the mission of providing information and/or services to the handicapped and their families. (See listing, beginning p. 000.) Those who intend to serve specific subgroups of exceptional children should find out about existing organizations and seriously consider affiliating with them. Many volunteer associations have well-designed printed material, taped public service announcements which can be made available to local radio and TV stations, and other resources for community education.

A few groups and associations which operate in almost every state are listed below. Others are listed at the end of this chapter. Comprehensive directories of groups dedicated to everything from autism to veterans are in the reference list. The services and activities of these organizations vary from one community to another. The descriptions are intended to be examples only, however, the examples of services are known to be offered in at least one community.

1. *The Association for Children with Learning Disabilities (ACLD)* develops improved educational techniques, programs, and services for children with learning disabilities. Most local groups are affiliated with International ACLD; funds come from donations and membership fees. The association provides publicity regarding learning problems, helps parents understand their children's learning problems, provides professionals with information on teaching and treatment, publishes a professional journal, and explores funding sources for programs. Local groups provide support to parents and professionals and often maintain resource lists for community services and tutors.

2. *Call for Action* is a national nonprofit referral and action service supported by local television and radio broadcasters. Volunteers help clients get access to services related to housing, welfare, consumer problems, drug abuse, taxes, health, Social Security, legal problems, utilities, licenses, records, permits, and education. They also offer follow-up services.

3. *The Easter Seal Society for Crippled Children and Adults* (NESS) is a voluntary health agency providing direct services in the rehabilitation of handicapped people. Funds come from an annual Easter Seal drive and private donations. The local agency may lend wheelchairs, hospital beds, and orthopedic appliances; it may furnish transportation to medical centers and special classes, if costs are reim-

bursed; it may provide camping facilities specially designed for disabled people. Other activities include information, referral and follow-up services, public education and advocacy, community recreational programs, and employment of handicapped individuals in Easter Seal Centers.

4. *The National Foundation—March of Dimes* offers programs of public health education, professional education, and medical services to fight against birth defects and their consequences. Its services are focused in three major areas: public education about birth defects; professional education; and medical services, including funding of clinical and research programs in maternal and child health, and some financial assistance to patients. Public education materials are available to everyone. The amount of financial assistance to patients with birth defects is determined in some communities by a volunteer board.

5. *The National Association for Mental Health* promotes good mental health and prevention and treatment of mental illness. Its activities include assessment of needs for treatment facilities and provisions for public education, as well as legislative monitoring and lobbying and client advocacy for the mentally ill. Local associations may provide volunteer services to patients and families. Educational programs are available to individuals, community and professional groups. The group attempts to identify unmet community mental health needs and to meet those needs. Membership is unrestricted.

6. *The National Association for Retarded Citizens* (NARC) is an advocacy organization which promotes the wellbeing of all mentally retarded citizens; fosters the development of programs ranging from research on mental retardation, to direct service for retarded people; helps parents to coordinate efforts on behalf of their children; promotes public understanding of mental retardation, and cooperation among agencies and professional groups to improve the life chances of retarded individuals; and solicits and disseminates funds for accomplishing these purposes.

7. *The National Association for Hearing and Speech Action* (NAHSA) is a subsidiary of the American Speech–Language–Hearing Association. It has a significant history as an advocacy organization for individuals handicapped by communication disorders. Its corporate structure permits inclusion of commercial, lay, and professional members, who advocate for quality programs for those with communication disorders. NAHSA provides information to the public, and maintains liaison with other national and international organizations with similar interests.

8. *Other organizations.* In recent years, many organizations have recognized that they can make important contributions to the overall wellbeing of disabled children and youth. For example, the Boy Scouts of America have well-developed programs and materials for retarded Scouts. YM- and YWCA services for the handicapped are available in many areas. United Way campaigns in many communities serve as a unifying force for citizens who wish to make contributions to disabled people.

COMMUNITY RESOURCES: SERVICES
FOR HANDICAPPED ADULTS

Sometimes members of a community overlook the very real, more ordinary needs of handicapped adults and their families. For example, a minister asked a young adult Sunday School class for volunteers to be overnight caretakers for a twenty-one-year-old, wheelchair-bound youth while his parents attended an out-of-town meeting. No one volunteered. That community needed a well-organized system of respite care for adults and families.

In most chronically handicapping conditions, handicapped individuals don't become unhandicapped when they become adults. The needs of handicapped adults may, in fact, be more acute; they are no longer cute little children who can be carried about. The friendly grin of childhood can become a bizarre leer in the eyes of other adults.

Two adult services which can be tapped by many communities are presented below:

1. *State Divisions of Vocational Rehabilitation* (DVR) designate appropriate agencies to provide services to individuals who are vocationally handicapped by a physical or mental disability. They help handicapped adolescents and adults obtain employment and training to utilize other therapeutic services, and provide examinations to determine extent of disability, work capacity, and possibility for improvement. They may also provide medical services to reduce handicaps; give counseling in selecting job objectives; furnish appliances such as limbs, hearing aids, and braces; conduct evaluation and training skills for employment; offer maintenance and transportation during training; provide tools and equipment for employment; and find job placements and do follow-up after placement.

2. *Goodwill Industries of America* provides employment and training for handicapped people in stores all over the country, where the public may buy reconditioned furniture, clothing, and housewares. It provides evaluation and counseling, vocational training, job placement, and sheltered employment. Eligibility is unrestricted for handicapped adults.

COMMUNITY RESOURCES: PROFESSIONALS

Several kinds of professionals, together with their training and their wide range of services; are described below. The alphabetical descriptions are concerned primarily with the professionals' roles in helping handicapped clients. Often these professionals will form a diagnostic and treatment team for an individual patient.

1. An *audiologist* tests for degree and type of hearing loss; determines what a person can and cannot hear; gives information on hearing loss associated with structural or auditory nerve impairment or associated with comprehending sound; advises on fitting and care of hearing aids and on rehabilitation of hearing-impaired people; and plans programs of hearing loss prevention and hearing conservation in industry and other settings where people are exposed to damaging levels of sound. Professional training includes the study of normal hearing and auditory perception, the physics of sound, and complex methods of testing. A master's degree is the minimum educational level; increasing numbers of audiologists have doctorates. Many states require licenses for audiologists. *All* handicapped children need an audiological assessment as part of a complete evaluation, because "hidden," inapparent auditory disorders often exist.

2. A *dentist* performs screening, diagnosis, and treatment of diseases. disorders, and accidents affecting the mouth, teeth, and all tissues of the mouth including gums and bones. Dentists may administer medication to prevent or treat illness related to dental problems. Further, a dentist may conduct continuing research in pain management, provide treatment which promotes normal facial growth and prevents deterioration of facial structures in disorders such as cleft palate, or treat epileptic children, who may develop gum disorders related to seizure-control medication. Dental care teams may include dental assistants, who work directly with dentists, and dental hygienists, who are licensed to clean teeth independently. Dental

specialties include general dentistry, orthodontia, periodontics, endodontics, pedodontia, prosthodontics, forensic dentistry and oral surgery. Dental services are often available in hospitals and public health facilities, as well as in private practice settings.

3. *Educators* teach academic and social skills in regular classes, special schools, hospitals, institutions and other settings. They may be certified as regular classroom teachers, special educators, or in high school by subject matter. With "mainstreaming" of handicapped children, regular classroom teachers and special educators plan together for the least restrictive educational alternatives in placing exceptional children in school settings where they learn best. Certified teachers have bachelor's degrees and some have master's degrees. Educators who specialize in teacher training and program development may hold doctoral degrees.

4. The *nurse* is traditionally thought of as the lady in white who cares for patients in a hospital. However, both male and female nurses work in many agencies. Public health nurses, for example, may make home visits, identify family health needs, teach maternal and child care, or facilitate delivery of a variety of health care services for children and families. Nurses are trained at several levels, ranging from two years of post-high school study through the master's degree. The trend is toward the bachelor's degree as minimal requirement for registered nurses (R.N.s). All nurses are licensed; licensed practical nurses (L.P.N.s) work under the supervision of R.N.s. Their level of training usually dictates the independence with which nurses may carry out health care activities. Among nursing roles which require specialized advanced training are the family nurse practitioner, nurse midwife, and clinical specialist.

5. The *nutritionist* evaluates a person's eating habits, nutritional status, and nutritional needs, counsels about normal nutrition for good general health, and about therapeutic nutrition for those on special diets. Nutritionists have a necessary role in diet planning for diabetic children, and for children with other disorders requiring careful diet control. Nutritionists may provide assistance with special feeding equipment and techniques that increase self-feeding skills and maintain adequate food consumption. Professional training includes studies in biochemistry, behavioral science, and efficient meal planning and preparation. A registered dietician (R.D.) or a nutritionist has a bachelor's degree or a master's degree, depending on the work setting, and will have completed an internship and passed a registration examination.

6. *Occupational therapists* (occupation here refers to activities and tasks that individuals must perform in daily living) evaluate and help children and adults to function at levels of maximum independence by learning to perform self-help tasks such as eating, bathing, dressing, talking, and playing, and in performing school tasks such as writing, cutting, and drawing. For example, they may train handicapped children in perceptual-motor skills, such as eye-hand coordination. Their services are provided in homes, hospitals, special schools, nursing homes, employment settings, and increasingly in public schools. There are two levels of O.T. personnel: Occupational Therapy Assistant, Certified (C.O.T.A.), and Occupational Therapist, Registered (O.T.R.). The registered O.T. has at least a bachelor's degree and field experience, and has passed national examinations.

7. The *optometrist* is a doctor of optometry, licensed to measure vision and to treat defects by prescribing corrective lenses and other optical aids, and by designing programs of eye exercises. This professional may specialize in developmental vision and visual perception problems related to learning disabilities. In some states, optometrists may use diagnostic and therapeutic drugs in treating patients. They also screen patients for disorders and diseases of the eye, and refer patients with such problems to an ophthalmologist (described under "physician").

8. *Physical therapists* are trained to evaluate and treat medically referred patients to prevent or relieve disability and pain, restore impaired movement and activity, promote healing, and teach adaptation to permanent disability. They evaluate joint mobility, muscle tone, strength and endurance, movement, walking, fit of braces and artificial limbs, and heart and lung functions. They are concerned with patients' sensation and perception and with their abilities in daily living activities. Qualifications include at least a bachelor's degree from an accredited program and passing a licensing examination.

9. The *physician*. By the time a handicapped child is three years old, he or she may have been evaluated by half a dozen physicians from several medical specialties. A few of the more common specialists who often have direct contact with handicapped patients are listed below:

Hematologists specialize in the study of blood, its components, and blood-forming tissues. A child with leukemia is under the continuing care of a hematologist.

Neurologists specialize in diagnosing and treating disorders of the brain and nervous system; a *neurosurgeon* operates on the brain and nervous system. Cerebral-palsied children, mentally retarded individuals, people with epilepsy, sometimes learning disabled individuals, and others may be treated by a neurologist.

Ophthalmologists specialize in the diagnosis and medical treatment of diseases and defects of the eye. Cerebral-palsied and mentally retarded individuals, for example, often have disorders of eye movement and visual perception. Children who had rubella (German measles) before they were born may need continuing vision care; diabetic children are a risk for visual disorders.

Orthopedists specialize in the preservation and treatment of function of the skeleton and associated structures. Cerebral-palsied children often have continuing contact with orthopedists.

The *otolaryngologist* specializes in diagnosis and treatment of diseases and disorders of the ear, nose, and throat (this specialty is often referred to as E.N.T.). Hearing-impaired individuals are under the care of an otolaryngologist, who may prescribe medication or perform surgery to correct some types of hearing disorders.

Pediatricians specialize in health care and treatment of diseases and disorders of children; the pediatrician monitors child development in handicapped and normal children.

The *physiatrist* specializes in physical medicine and rehabilitation, with training in medicine, physiology, pathology, pharmacology, and behavioral sciences.

The *psychiatrist* is a physician trained in the branch of medicine which studies, treats, and prevents mental illness. Psychiatrists treat children and adults whose responses to life stresses affect both mental and physical health. They may prescribe medication to ease symptoms, and are often concerned with relationships between physical and mental health, and with the psychological correlates of physical disorders. Not all are in office practice; many specialize in community psychiatry, psycho-pharmacology, forensic psychiatry, and in other areas.

10. The *psychologist* has a master's degree or doctorate in psychology, a behavioral science which studies mental processes and behavior. Psychologists may provide psychotherapy; may evaluate both normal and abnormal behaviors and feelings; and may use tests to assess behavior, intellect, personality, and achievement of normal and exceptional individuals. Practitioners who offer treatment are licensed in most states as *clinical* psychologists or *counseling* psychologists. Psychologists may be trained in many subspecialties, such as social psychology, experimental psychology, developmental psychology, school psychology and others.

11. The *therapeutic recreation specialist* plans and directs rec-

reational activities for people who are recovering from physical or mental illness or who are coping with disability. Activities are based on the enjoyable use of leisure time in promoting the mental and physical well-being of handicapped people, through restoring self-confidence, increasing interpersonal interaction, and developing avocations for permanent enrichment. A college degree from an accredited program is the minimum requirement. A master's degree with emphasis on therapeutic recreation is the optimal level of preparation. Junior or community colleges have programs for *therapeutic recreation aides*.

12. *Rehabilitation counselors* evaluate and guide handicapped adults through all major phases of the rehabilitation process. They help to obtain vocational rehabilitation, training, education or therapy, government benefits, access to community facilities, recreation, and devices which contribute to independent living. They can also identify special needs of disabled adults and help them understand the need for assistance, and act to coordinate various services. Essential preparation for counseling is at the graduate level.

13. *Social workers* are employed in social service agencies, child care facilities, hospitals, schools, diagnostic centers, and numerous other settings. They may provide individual or family therapy to help people adjust to the changed life roles and new demands a handicapped person places on a family, and may serve as facilitators and liaison agents to help families utilize appropriate services. Although some social workers have bachelor's degrees, the accepted national standard is a master's degree in social work, the M.S.W.

14. The *Speech—language pathologist* is a specialist in human communication, its normal development and its disorders. He or she is trained to conduct screening and diagnosis, and to plan programs of therapy for individuals with communication disorders. This professional may assess handicapped persons to determine whether they use oral language appropriate for their ages. Speech—language pathologists work in schools, rehabilitation centers, health departments, hospitals, nursing care facilities, community clinics, private practice, colleges and universities, and other agencies. They are often called "speech clinicians," and were formerly called "speech therapists." A few individuals with bachelor's degrees continue to work in some settings. The national standards are a master's degree and the Certificate of Clinical Competence granted by the American Speech-Language-Hearing Association (ASHA). Licensing is required in some states.

Other professions. Numerous other specialists may participate in the treatment and rehabilitation of disabled children and adults. Descriptions of roles and professional training of those listed below may be found in the *Disability and Rehabilitation Handbook* (1978) listed at the end of this chapter.

Art therapist	Manual arts therapist
Biomedical engineer	Medical and dental assistants
Corrective specialist	Music therapist
Dance therapist	Orientation and mobility
Educational therapist	instructor
Genetic ounselor	Orthotist
Homemaker-home	Osteopathic physician
health aide	Podiatrist
Industrial therapist	Prosthetist
Laboratory technicians	Respiratory therapist

The *Handbook* also contains detailed descriptions of many kinds of disabling conditions and rehabilitation facilities. It provides a comprehensive directory of advocacy organizations, federal agencies, periodicals, materials and equipment. This volume would be a useful addition to a religious or community organization's library.

COMMUNITY RESOURCES: HOW TO FIND THEM

Sometimes locating resources and finding out who is eligible for services can present problems. Some communities develop excellent communication networks for helping families find appropriate help. For example, in one county in a southeastern state, the County Mental Health Association and the Commission for Women jointly published a guide to all family resources in the county. Harriette Hitt, former chair of the Orange County, N.C., Commission for Women, observes that readily available information services can keep a problem from being a crisis ("Orange County Family Resources," 1980–81). Readily available information can reduce the stress of making important decisions and can help professionals provide better services.

However, less formal strategies for finding community services are available and readily accessible to any citizen:

The telephone book. Business or professional customers of the telephone company are included in the Yellow Pages alphabetically by type of service, profession, or product. Yellow Pages headings are con-

sistent in all phone books. Questions about whether an agency is duly
licensed should be directed to governmental authorities responsible for
regulating such businesses or professions.

A trick in using the Yellow Pages is to make a list of key words
which are related to the nature of the problem to be solved. Some
examples of key words with corresponding Yellow Pages directory headings are listed below.

Alcoholic rehabilitation	Psychologists
Audiologists	Reading Instruction
Dentists	Social Service Organizations
Marriage and family counseling	Social Workers
Mental retardation	Speech Pathologists
Psychiatrists	

Citizens from small towns may check the phone book in larger
communities to find numerous resources available to eligible persons
regardless of place of residence.

The white pages listings are alphabetical by names of organizations or businesses. More precise information about names of agencies,
individuals, or professionals is required in order to find specific help.

Armed only with the name of a city or county, the caller may find
phone numbers and addresses for dozens of agencies and departments.
In one community, the following subheadings were found under the
listing of "_____, County of":

Health Department	Mental Health
Children's Clinic	Adolescent Group Home
Family Planning	Mental Retardation and
	Developmental Disabilities

In another community, the Inter-Faith Council for Social Services
had compiled a list of "Community Service Numbers," which appears in
the phone directory just before the white pages. Headings on the list
include:

Aging Services	Learning Disabilities
Alcoholism	Legal Assistance
Blind Services	Child Abuse
Crisis Counseling	Mental Health Services

Day Care   Mental Retardation Services
Drug Abuse   Physically Handicapped Services
Home Health Care   Volunteer Opportunities

Developing such a list of community agencies where one doesn't exist, and arranging for its publication, would be an appropriate project for a religious or volunteer group. The telephone company takes no responsibility for errors or omissions in such a list, but provides space in the phone book to increase telephone access to service agencies.

UTILIZING COMMUNITY RESOURCES:
HOW TO MAKE A REFERRAL

A religious education teacher or a teacher in a church-sponsored pre-school could be the first objective observer to suspect that a child is developmentally delayed in motor skills, language development, or socially appropriate behavior. However, talking to parents about the "differences" of their small child can be anxiety-producing for everybody, particularly if the concerned adult is not in a position of authority.

What to Say. There is no one way to approach parents about referring their child for special help, but some strategies seem to work better than others. One approach is for concerned adults to focus on their need for help rather than on the child's shortcomings: "Let me mention something to you. We have a hard time understanding Bobby. He has lots of good things to say, but we need some help in planning activities that can help him be a good talker. We also need some help in planning playtime activities that aren't too rambunctious. What would you think of our scheduling a speech checkup at the Developmental Evaluation Clinic?" This strategy has a very different focus from making everything Bobby's responsibility: "Bobby can't talk plain," or "Bobby gets frustrated when we can't understand him," or "Bobby is terrified of the jungle gym."

Often the parent who is angered by such information ultimately seeks help, so it's worth taking a chance, if the concerned adult can remain objective.

Parents of older children, or of small children with more severe exceptionalities, may be "old pros" at utilizing community resources. A reasonable approach to parents of these children is: "Have you been able to find the help you need in our town? Can we help you find other services?"

Whom to contact. Deciding whom to call is sometimes easier if the referral focuses on client/family characteristics, rather than on agency/service characteristics. If parents can accept referral for one aspect of the problem, regardless of the severity of the other aspects of the disability, this dimension of the disorder provides entry into the service system. Eddy and his family are a case in point.

A call came to a speech and hearing center from a minister. He said, "I'm Roger _____, pastor of _____ Church. May I make an appointment for Eddy _____? The parents are in our congregation, and they are really fine people. Eddy is five years old, and his speech is really strange." The receptionist asked the minister to accompany the family when they came to the center since it was apparent that they trusted him.

On the day of the appointment, as the center staff chatted informally with the family, they recognized that Eddy had many of the characteristics of severe autism. His "echoic" language — parroting television commercials—was one outstanding symptom of this complex disorder. Eddy's parents used the word *autistic,* but they focused on the communication disorder. Eddy's father said, "He'd be okay if he could just talk right."

The staff discussed a therapy plan to be undertaken, with the family's full knowledge that other specialists' evaluations must be part of a comprehensive and ethical procedure. The procedure was nevertheless devised to prevent patient "fragmentation."

The conference with Eddy's parents went something like this: "You're right. Eddy should be talking like other five-year-olds. If you want us to, we'll take Eddy in therapy for six months. During that time we will get to know Eddy, and just as importantly, we'll get to know you. We believe that we can all make better decisions if we have some extended time together. We will call in other people to help us make good decisions."

Eddy's mother's relieved response was, "Somebody is finally going to try to help us. You're not sending us away."

Church members helped with transportation, and Eddy never missed a therapy session.

During the six months a psychologist, a social worker, a pediatrician, and an audiologist evaluated Eddy. He had well-planned language therapy and was eventually able to sit with a group of preschoolers.

The outcome was that his parents, surrounded by support, were able to make unhurried decisions about placing Eddy in a residential treatment center.

The minister had taken the first crucial step by helping the family to enter the system where they were *able* to enter. The professional staff handled the next steps in the referral process.

With the family or client-centered approach to the question of whom to call, the referring person is not required to make detailed clinical decisions in trying to choose the right agency for a specific disorder.

An adult referral illustrates another example of a "client-centered" rather than an "agency-centered" referral:

A young foreign social workers with ambitions to become a minister was on an eight-month study assignment in the United States. The young man had very poor dental health and severe dental malocclusion of the type commonly called "underbite." His host "mother and father" discussed strategies for talking with the young man about his dental health and the social and professional disadvantages of the problem. Finally, the host "mother" faced the problem directly. She said, "José, I want to talk to you about something serious. I want to talk with you about your teeth. Would you like me to take you to a dentist?" José paused and then said softly, "Oh, would you? I was afraid to ask." Then he laughed and said, "You were so serious! I thought maybe I had done something dreadful like go to bed with my shoes on!"

The host "mother" took José to a free walk-in dental clinic staffed by young dental interns. They cleaned his teeth, and began a program of dental education and restoration and planned for financing for full-mouth restoration in a university dental clinic.

José's host "mother" helped José enter the system at a level which he could accept. Joe entered divinity school, married, and got major dental rehabilitation—all within one year.

What to say to the agency. In making a referral to any agency, the caller should always give his or her name and some identifying information. The opening statements of the minister who referred Eddy are exactly right.

The person who makes a referral should be prepared with certain information and questions and should take notes on the answers. Examples of information to have ready:

1. Name of child or adult
2. Date of birth
3. Address/phone number

4. Name of parent or guardian
5. Name of school and teacher (or type of employment)
6. Name of caller and relationship to client
7. Phone number of contact person
8. Brief statement of reason for referral

Practices vary from one agency to another, but some basic principles underlie scheduling, treatment, and training in most agencies. Some appropriate questions include the following:

1. Is an appointment necessary? Some agencies offer "walk-in" or "call-in" clinics; others have strict appointment schedules.

2. Does the agency require that parents or guardians make direct contact, or may another person (clergy, social worker, pediatrician, nurse, family friend) make appointments?

3. Does the agency require that application forms be returned before an appointment is scheduled? What are the implications of this requirement? Who can fill out the case history form? Mother? Teenage sister? A volunteer?

4. What fees are involved? Who pays the fees?

5. Does this agency cooperate with other agencies such as Easter Seals? Crippled Children's Services?

6. Do families provide their own transportation?

A note on transportation. Transportation is one of the simplest and yet most persistent problems families face in obtaining successful long-term service. Despite America's continuing love affair with the automobile, not everybody has a car. Individuals with chronic conditions often need dependable transportation for months or years. As in Eddy's case described above, religious and volunteer groups are in a unique position to organize transportation.

The referral process does not stop with the initial visit to a service agency. Those who take the responsibility of starting the helping process are well advised to assist with follow-through, so that continuing services can be just that—continuing.

THE EXTENDED COMMUNITY: SPECIAL
SCHOOLS AND INSTITUTIONS

There has been much discussion in recent years about what is now called "deinstitutionalization." This term has unfortunately been narrowed only to mean "taking people out of institutions." A social worker specializing in institutional care for children pointed out that the word "deinstitutionalize" has a broader meaning. The institution may deinstitutionalize activities and behaviors of residents, so that they can become independent from the institution in making their own phone calls, choosing their own clothing, and in making the numerous daily decisions most people make automatically. A group home with only six residents may be so rigidly structured that residents engage in "institutional" behavior and develop no skills for independent decision-making.

Whatever the reasons and social forces at work, residential facilities and institutions continue to shelter the disabled of every age and disability. Occasionally newspapers, movies, or television feature a sensational, tragic story about abuse of patients in so-called "warehouses" for the disabled. Unfortunately, these isolated stories may be true; however, the fact remains that most psychiatrists, psychologists, social workers, clergy, aides, and child care workers in such institutions are not bumbling, insightless monsters. Most of them are caring, competent people who are good at their jobs.

Special schools and, yes, *institutions* may be the "best" alternatives for some handicapped individuals and their families. Concerned adults may be supportive of families' rights to choose residential placement for their family member if that solution helps them cope better with life stresses and with other family obligations. A viable family unit should not be sacrificed for the sake of one deviant member with a limited future. The decision to utilize institutional services should be honored without stigma.

Families rarely make decisions to place relatives in homes, special schools or institutions without agonizing about whether they're making the right decision. They may experience guilt and renewed grief about the thwarted, foiled life for which they feel responsible. A prominent physician in a mid-western community sought the counsel of a social worker on the staff of a hospital. He wept as he described his retarded granddaughter and "my daughter, my little girl, who has to cope with this damaged child. Have we done the right thing to place Elizabeth in the state training school?" The social worker met with the daughter and granddaughter the next time Elizabeth came home for a visit. The social worker's final opinion was that the family had chosen wisely in placing the little girl. The decisions had been appropriate for the child and the family in that situation at that time.

Choosing Special Placement. Accurate information is a most powerful tool in helping families with decisions about choosing special care facilities.

The *Directory for Exceptional Children* (Bringardner, 1978) is a resource for parents, community volunteers, and professionals. The listings encompass public and private residential schools and day care facilities serving children who have a broad range of developmental and behavioral handicaps. The book also contains a wealth of information on associations and public funding resources dedicated to disabled and handicapped individuals.

PROGRAMS FOR HANDICAPPED PRESCHOOLERS

Public schools have a mandate to provide education to all handicapped children of school age. Religious and other agencies have an honorable tradition of providing preschool and day care services for children during the preschool years.

1. *Head Start.* Project Head Start was launched as a national program of comprehensive developmental services for preschool children from low-income families. Programs tailored to the needs of individual communities and individual children implement the congressional mandate that at least ten percent of Head Start enrollment be available for handicapped children.

Project Head Start has developed an excellent series of eight manuals, *Mainstreaming Preschoolers,* available to any interested citizen. The manuals are for sale from the Superintendent of Documents, U.S. Government Printing Office, Washington, D.C. 20402. Order stock number 017-092-00029-4.

2. *Preschool and Day Care.* The name *preschool* often implies that there is educational content in a childcare program. Some day care settings, particularly those for handicapped children, may also have educational and therapeutic programs; however, "day care" often means simply care provided during the day; some children are also in "night care" programs. As more mothers work outside the home and as extended families are dispersed in distant locations, day care and preschool services have become important community resources.

Handicapped preschoolers need appropriate early childhood learning experiences just as nondisabled children do. It is inappropriate, and in some states illegal, for religious or other volunteer organizations to set up day care or preschool programs which do not meet rather stringent guidelines for optimum child learning and child safety. In the late 1970s, twelve states required certification for teachers of handicapped preschool children (Kirk and Gallagher, 1979).

Some states have standards for childcare facilities which define different classifications of care depending on length of time children are in the facility, number of children in care, staff-child ratios, and ages of children. The classifications include the *registered* day care home, *licensed* day care facility, and *certified* child care facility.

Community groups can usually obtain information on day care facilities and requirements for programs from the Department of Social Services. Guidelines and/or laws exist in areas such as safety and fire protection, naptime arrangements, food preparation, play and learning materials, characteristics of staff, and availability of other therapeutic staff.

Day care, preschool and Head Start programs are in the business of *preventing* handicaps. There is accumulating evidence that children with good early childhood and intervention programs are better employees in their teen years. Furthermore, there seems to be a decrease in delinquent behavior among those who have positive early childhood experiences. There is additional evidence that families whose children have "the odds against them" may learn to hold their children in higher regard if the children participate in early intervention programs. Despite some criticism to the contrary, preschool and early childhood programs do not reduce family cohesiveness (Schweinhart and Weikart 1980).

COMMUNITY NEEDS

One way to approach the question of community need is to determine how many people have what kinds of problems. What are the incidence (new cases) and prevalence (prevailing cases) of various disabilities and the kinds of populations in which they occur? The incidence of childhood arthritis is low. The prevalence is higher because children with the disorder accumulate in the population.

Overall prevalence of mental retardation in the U. S. is about three percent. Stedman (1970) developed tables of prevalence of mental retardation in four different, hypothetical communities of 100,000 people each. In suburbia the prevalence of mental retardation is estimated to be about two percent; in the inner cities the prevalence is about seven percent.

Estimates of the prevalence of learning disabilities range from one to ten percent. About three percent seems to be the rate with which educators are most comfortable. The fact that the male-to-female ratio seems to be about five to one would suggest that a community might provide a young man as a counselor for learning disabled children.

Hearing impairment is a disability which illustrates changing prevalence patterns and their impact on service planning. Something over 6 percent of Americans of all ages are estimated to have hearing impairment severe enough to impair communication. In 1964, following a major rubella (German measles) epidemic, thousands (estimates range from 20,000 to 200,000) of hearing- and/or vision-impaired babies were born to mothers who had rubella during early pregnancy. By the time these babies were three years old in 1967, preschools for hearing-impaired, multihandicapped children had sprung up like mushrooms in scores of communities across the country. Then came another major event with far-reaching implications: in 1969 a rubella vaccine was licensed. There will probably never be another "epidemic" of hearing-impaired preschoolers who require such a massive mobilization of community resources in health and education.

In 1969, one city of 100,000 had a preschool deaf program serving fifteen preschoolers. Ten years later, the school system had one deaf preschooler, a sprinkling of hearing-impaired elementary children from a five county area, and twelve deaf junior high school students. In the early 1980s, the rubella babies had become teenagers.

Does the community need trained teachers of the deaf? Do needs lie in training vocational rehabilitation counselors? Do these needs change?

MOBILIZING A COMMUNITY

In the 1970s, disabled individuals became increasingly vocal on their own behalf. In 1981, the United Nations specially designated Year of the Disabled Person, positive attention was focused on this special population. Legislation, consumer rights, and other agents of change have been mobilized for disabled children and adults. Community mobilization for exceptional populations can take many forms. One community's efforts are described below.

The Whole Person, Inc. in Kansas City, Missouri (see resources listing, beginning p. 000), is a clearinghouse in a metropolitan area assisting those with mental or physical disabilities to bring together ablebodied persons who serve as advocates to enhance the lifestyles of disabled persons. The Whole Person provides channels of communication among groups and individuals in the disabled community. It unites to speak for the disabled community to news media, the legislature, and special interest groups. It advocates for rights in housing, employment, recreation, and education.

MOBILIZING COMMUNITY VOLUNTEERS

Volunteering is a happy American pastime. Many of the organizations mentioned in this chapter are staffed by volunteers. Gray Ladies, Candy Stripers, scouts, civic clubs, and Interfaith Councils are but a few of the volunteer groups which improve services in a host of agencies.

The path for those who volunteer to help the handicapped can be fraught with pitfalls. Untrained volunteers often want to provide direct therapy, tutoring, or "laying on of hands." They may propose simplistic solutions for complex problems: "My daughter will come home from college in May. Can she tutor these retarded children this summer?" "One of our temple members is a retired English teacher. Can she help this child with his speech?" "We've got a high chair we can strap this cerebral-palsied child into." "After Grandpa died we kept his hearing aid. The batteries are corroded in it, but we'll clean it up and give it to Glenda."

A good heart and a love of children do not unfortunately equip a college junior to plan and carry out successful educational strategies appropriate to the needs of retarded learners, or a retired English teacher to identify the complexities of a communication disorder and to develop appropriate therapy. Grandpa's hearing aid may be wrong for Glenda.

Those who ask "What can we do to help?" should remember that it is illegal in some states for anyone other than licensed professionals to provide various kinds of therapy. Home or school practice may be appropriate; often such supportive efforts make progress possible. However, untrained helpers without clearly formulated goals and objectives, based on well-founded theory and an understanding of disorders, may waste the time and motivation of everybody.

Barry, a gifted ten year old, had a severe stuttering problem which was socially and academically handicapping. He had had three years of "therapy" provided by a tutor who sought to help Barry's stuttering by improving his feelings about himself, and by providing a "successful social experience." These are laudable goals. They usually do not change stuttering. The tutor declared Barry to be unmotivated and disinterested. Barry was resistant to formal speech therapy. He regarded himself as a failure with regard to speech change. He agreed to give formal therapy a try — for one summer. At the end of therapy with a certified speech clinician, Barry's speech was within normal limits. In talking with a group of university graduate students, Barry stated, "For three years I worked on my feelings. This summer I worked on my speech and I *feel* better about it!"

Successful volunteer programs may have several components:

1. Get information from qualified professionals or organizations
2. Adapt the information to a specific community
3. Learn about laws governing services to the handicapped
4. Aim toward developing programs which employ trained professionals who help volunteers learn what they need to know.

The late Dr. John Cassel, a world-renowned public health physician and epidemiologist, used to say, "The more you know about something, the harder it is to make it simple." The converse of this may be, "The less you know about something, the easier it is to oversimplify." Those who want to help should set about learning about handicapped people, their clinical characteristics, their health problems, their learning strengths and weaknesses, and their phenomenal diversity. An educator discussed getting well-trained people to teach handicapped children: "Competent teachers are like well-trained ballet dancers. They make it look graceful and easy."

Obviously, not everything which helps exceptional children is carried out by professional people. Parents give daily medication for seizures or diabetes; sister is the "teacher" for language practice; college students provide practice sessions in reading; Boy Scouts help in "wheelies" sports for friends in wheelchairs; scores of volunteers plan the Special Olympics. The fact remains that the best help is that which is designed by professionals as being appropriate to the needs of individuals, their particular deficits, and the community in which they live.

Screening a community or group of people for a disorder is a specific example of an appropriate volunteer service, and yet volunteer screening must be utilized with caution. Screening is the process of identifying a disorder or problem or potential problem. *Diagnosis* is the process of establishing the distinguishing characteristics and detailed manifestations of a disorder, so that appropriate treatment may be developed. Screening had formal mandate in the 1967 amendment to the Social Security Act, which required early and periodic screening, diagnosis, and treatment (EDSDT) programs for all children receiving Medicaid. These efforts to find young handicapped children are predicated on the belief that services initiated early in life can improve life chances and can help prevent secondary conditions which confound some handicaps (Kirk and Gallagher, 1979).

Since the sheer limitation of numbers makes it impossible for professionals to screen all children for all disorders, community and religious groups are sometimes mobilized to screen for some kinds of disorders. Screening by community groups can be a double-edged sword. Inexperienced screeners or inaccurate screening devices may overload diagnostic services by identifying too many "false positives"— i.e., incorrectly interpreting testing results to show a problem exists when it does not. Conversely, they may identify individuals as not having a disorder when in fact disorders exist ("false negatives"), thereby denying treatment or educational programs where they are needed. In one town retired citizens set up a blood pressure screening station at a yard sale in a church parking lot. No one had determined whether the elderly screeners had hearing acuity good enough to obtain accurate blood pressure readings. Some strange results were obtained.

In Isaiah 65:23, the people of Jerusalem are described: "They shall not labor in vain, or bear children for calamity." The parents of exceptional children, like the people of Jerusalem, do not bear nor rear their offspring to be children for calamity. Calamity can be averted for exceptional children by an objective well-informed citizenry working to develop services appropriate to the needs of those who will use them.

REFERENCES

Bringardner, A. *Directory for Exceptional Children.* 8th ed. Boston: Porter Sargeant, 1978.

Goldenson, R. M., Dunham, J. R., and Dunham, C. S. *Disability and Rehabilitation Handbook.* New York: McGraw-Hill, 1978.

Kirk, S. A., and Gallagher, J. J. *Educating Exceptional Children.* Boston: Houghton Mifflin, 1979.

Lynch, E. W., Simms, B. H., von Hippel, C. S., and Shuchat, J. *Mainstreaming Preschoolers: Children with Mental Retardation.* Washington, D.C.: Department of Health, Education, and Welfare (Publications No. OHDS 78-31110), 1978.

Orange County, N.C., Mental Health Association (333 McMasters Street, Chapel Hill, N.C. 27514) and Orange County Commission for Women (131 Court Street, Hillsborough, N.C. 27278). "Orange County Family Resources," 1981.

Schweinhart, L. J. and Weikart, D. P. "Young Children Grow Up: The Effects of the Perry Preschool Program on Youths Through Age Fifteen." Monograph no. 7. Ypsilanti, Mich.: High/Scope Educational Research Foundation, 1980.

7
Pastoral Help for Families of Handicapped Children

John R. Ball

THE BIRTH OF A CHILD is a very special event, engaging the excited interest of friends, family members, and often members of the parents' religious community.

For the father and mother, there have been weeks and months of hope, anxiety, planning and finally, joy. But when the infant is born with a significant health problem or a serious handicapping condition, there is a sense of bewilderment. What does this mean for the parents, and their friends and family? What does it mean to the church or synagogue? For some, the church or temple is a part of the extended family and constitutes a caring community. Within that context the congregation leader has a definite responsibility—that of helping to care for the family.

In the Christian church, which constitutes my own particular frame of reference, we have specific theological perceptions of the child. We feel that every child is born in the "image of God." This tends to suggest some specific levels of perfection and requires very definite commitments from parents to such potential. When that perfection appears to be absent, parents may question themselves and God's love. Facing such imperfection may call the theological proposition of perfection into question. They may question the claim that all life has meaning and is an expression of God's love. If the new life is an expression of God's perfect love, then why this imperfect gift?

In attempting to respond to these questions, I will rely heavily on my own training and experience as a Christian minister in a Protestant church. It is my hope that leaders of congregations in other religious faiths will find these observations to be relevant to their own experiences with similar problems, problems which arise in every religious tradition.

A ROLE FOR THE CHURCH: OPPORTUNITY
AND OBLIGATION

As the pastor and the caring community consider what they can do to help, it is useful to understand the child within the context of the family. All members of the family are affected by a new birth. Their responses will vary according to their roles, degree of involvement, feelings and other factors, but everyone will react. Everyone in his or her own way will work to find ways of coping with this new experience, this difference that has entered the family's life. The pastor and other members of the church have an unusual opportunity to help families and themselves to find answers through a shared search.

Families are not always sure that pastors know how to help. When asked what she thought about the role of the pastor in helping families of handicapped children, a mother with an autistic teenager responded that she "had never thought about the possibility of receiving help from a pastor, although [she] had often thought about the services that could be provided by churches." This response came from a mother who is active in her church. She sings in the choir, and she and her family participate in other church activities. But she had not felt the presence of a caring and helpful pastor. The idea that there could be a pastoral role had not occurred to her, even though her family have been members of several congregations during the life of their autistic son. This same mother went on to say, "One must consider what the capabilities and responsibilities of a pastor are. If a pastor is one who is able to provide counseling and support to those who are involved in a stressful situation, then a pastor could be of real help to families with handicapped children."

It is important to note that there is still a question in this mother's mind about whether or not a pastor can be of help; but if he or she can be, then the mother has very specific expectations. The needs of her family include the pastor because of the nature of the experience of a handicapped child and its implications for spiritual coping and growth. The experience penetrates every value and belief. The extent to which the church may become involved in helping families of handicapped children may be related to the caring capacity of the pastor and his or her training. The mother noted that the pastor would need some understanding of families with handicapped children, and an awareness of the continuing stress and anxiety, perplexity, spiritual questioning, and examination of personal values which they experience. Living with a handicapped child is like an unending crisis. It progresses through several stages and each stage presents new opportunities and challenges for the family and the church (see Chapter 3).

An average-size church will have one or more families with a handicapped child. When there is a handicapped member, the pastor will need special sensitivity to succeed in reaching the family. The pastor who chooses to see, hear and understand their needs and accept a partnership responsibility with them expands his or her ministry and deepens the life of the church as a caring community. The beginning of pastoral caring and sensitivity may be the willingness and ability to help parents assess their situation.

There are probably many reasons why parents and pastors often do not develop appropriate helping relationships. Many times the parents have had to accept the birth very quickly and have had to learn to cope very suddenly with caring for a child with many special needs. In having to adjust and function so quickly, they sometimes may present to the world an efficient and well-adjusted exterior that may be totally different from their inner feelings. Their well-adjusted façade may become burdensome for parents as they begin to be increasingly admired by their friends and neighbors for coping so well in such a difficult situation. Admiration by others may trap parents into feeling they must try to maintain a coping image. Even if they sometimes need to express pain or a lack of confidence, they hesitate to admit that their ability to function well is not as great as they would like. The pastor may misinterpret the parent's behavior because he or she wants to believe the parents are really doing well. Thinking that the parents are strong and equal to the problem may be unrealistic, but this kind of positive assumption is much more comforting than the difficulties that challenge one when the parents react openly and realistically to their difficulties. Therefore, it may be only too easy to fail to inquire sufficiently into the deep feelings that parents may be experiencing.

Recently, a pastor thought privately that a parent and fellow church member was displaying great weakness of character in dealing with a very difficult situation. On investigating the situation, the pastor learned that the mother had not been able to come to grips and accept a great trauma in her family. Several days passed before she was able to accept the love and reassurances of her friends to the point that she could once again resume a more normal existence. The pastor had made two vital misjudgments: neither the mother's character nor faith was weak simply because she needed time and counsel to be able to adjust to a difficult situation. The minister had an opportunity to be a vital part in that process of adjusting. Fortunately for the mother in distress, she had friends in the church with more sensitive insight concerning her needs in this particular situation. If the minister's initial perception of the situation had traveled very widely among his congregation, a number of members probably would never reveal to him any traces of inner turmoil for fear of being labeled "weak." His opportunities to serve were greatly diminished by his response. Attitudes of acceptance or rejection are contagious in a community. In the church community, the pastor is an important "carrier" whose ideas, values, and attitudes are usually transmitted rather effectively.

It would be meaningful if a pastor could sit down privately with parents and acknowledge that he or she admires them in their ability to function well in a difficult situation but would admire them no less if they occasionally found the going very rough and wanted to share it. It is true that the "squeaking wheel gets the grease," but the pastor must not miss the opportunity to serve the parent who is struggling courageously and is not "squeaking" in the process. Perhaps they need the opportunity to "squeak."

There are some fundamental and valued principles that will assist a minister in making sincere and directed efforts to help families with handicapped children. Self-study and an inventory of one's own strengths and weaknesses are important. One cannot see the strengths or accept the weaknesses of others without a knowledge and acceptance of one's own.

HELPING AS A DELIBERATE PROCESS

Preparing ourselves for supportive intervention involves thought in order for our best efforts to emerge. The pastor can burden parents by calling attention to their problems if he or she cannot suggest a way to lessen them. One also needs a careful and articulate acceptance of where a parent is in terms of the problem, with the careful pursuit of more appropriate and meaningful responses. It is never acceptable to say that someone is weak because his or her behavior is not perfectly matched with his or her needs. Consequently, the pastor must be capable of careful analysis of the issues and problems presented by the individual seeking help.

The church ministry is one of providing for other people. The ministry often focuses on human behavior in a group context, with limited opportunities for work with individuals. A pastor who is concerned with the personal needs of the congregation may become very frustrated with the organizational demands of the job which take away from individual counseling and working with families. There obviously has to be some balancing of the roles that a pastor must play, and there is no particular formula available to help determine the most efficient use of one's self and one's time.

In order to be sensitively responsive to the needs of families with handicapped children, the pastor needs both knowledge and specific skills. These include skills in problem solving, diagnosing, and counseling, as well as leadership abilities in order to promote programs within his church and in the larger community in which his church exists.

While the problems associated with the birth and rearing of a handicapped child are superficially obvious, the far-reaching implications of the problems are not so obvious in terms of their effects on individual families. Families bring different life experiences and consequently different kinds of coping abilities to any situation. But the pastor can help the family in choosing some part of its problem as a beginning place for work. It is essential that the pastor assist in finding a beginning resolution.

The ability to break down a problem into identifiable parts is an important skill in helping people. The full measure of any difficult or painful situation can be beyond a person's ability to withstand at one time. The burden of bearing a handicapped child is often too much for parents to adjust to all at once, and sometimes one can help them to approach the situation in parts for purposes of solving immediate problems. It may be helpful to the family if the pastor tries to identify specific problems. It may be perfectly acceptable for the pastor to ask the family what problems they can identify. They may present an array of problems; if so, ranking them in some sort of family priority may be helpful. From this effort may come a focal problem or one that has some immediate need or priority over others. This is not to say that any problem should be disregarded, but some are more pressing than others. It will usually help if the family can define its problems in specific, concrete terms. They may be asked to tell how a specific problem interferes with their family's functioning. They may need help in responding in specific, down-to-earth terms that can be managed.

After helping the family to define the problems, the pastor may be able to help them recognize that some have a more immediate need for resolution than others. The pastor should not presume that families are willing to work on a problem simply because it has been identified, but the pastor may serve a unique role in helping them to move through feelings of ambivalence to a commitment to begin resolution. Through dialogue a partnership may be established that will lead to problem resolution.

The pastor must be cautiously articulate in helping the family to identify problems. A focus must be maintained on what the family defines as their wants and needs without any imposition of the pastor's perceptions or analysis being presented. This is not to say that one should avoid using professional judgment, or perhaps risk showing feelings in assisting the family to select problems that are important and than can tolerate immediate emphasis. Be willing and ready to relate to the problem as the family sees it and be able to work from that beginning in partnership with the family. At the same time, exercise some caution in the commitments you make to resolving problems. If it is a problem beyond your capabilities or the means of your church, refer the family to the professional help needed and perhaps use your influence in the community to assist in securing that service.

The immediate responsibility may be to enter into a problem-solving process that will not only lead to resolution but also will help the family learn how to carry on their own problem-solving processes. There may not be a great deal that you can do to change the situation of the family with a handicapped child, but you can affect their well-being and management of the situation.

If the pastor is to be realistic about a family's ability to respond to its situation positively, he or she must realize that there will be some obstacles to their normal problem-solving efforts. These include the fact that very often external resources are not available. Only recently has public law mandated that society must provide for basic necessities such as education for all children. Even though the law makes such provision, we must not assume that such assistance is available. In some communities there will be insufficient medical expertise to provide treatment for the child, and there may be limited numbers of allied health personnel to help meet the child's needs adequately. It is also possible that many other kinds of community supports are not available, and traditionally the churches have had few services available for these families. We must realize that being unable to find help may deplete the family members emotionally and physically, and there may not be enough energy left to apply to the logical resolution of their many problems.

THE HELPING ROLE OF THE PASTOR

We have discussed the fact that the problems of the handicapped child are of long duration, have many phases, and may be sufficiently stressful that the family becomes victims of emotions which govern their thinking and actions. Some parents bog down because they have never developed systematic strategies of thinking and planning. It may be a long time before they are equal to the requirements for effective parenting of a handicapped child. A natural process of identifying obstacles should occur before the pastor makes any assumptions about the ability of the family to cope or to solve problems. The pastor has an unusual opportunity to share with the family in their emotional and spiritual growth as they learn to meet the long-term needs of their handicapped child.

As has been suggested, one of the important roles the pastor can play with the family is that of teacher of the process of problem solving. Perlman (1957, pp. 60–61) has found that the essential characteristics of problem solving are: (1) ascertaining and clarifying the facts of the problem; (2) thinking through the facts; and (3) making choices or decisions.

It is often useful to record your findings as you assist the family in the problem-solving process. Even though you may think that you know the family, you should collect as many facts as possible about their situation. If you are not knowledgeable about the nature of the handicapping condition, you need to become so in order to understand better the child's needs and the demands on the family. An understanding of the relationships of family members to each other and the relationship of the family to its environment is essential if you are to have some understanding of the dynamic interaction of the handicapped child, family, and environment.

If you succeed in understanding the family, your evaluation will have a level of precision that comes from systematic observation and assessment. In this effort you will also receive some direction from the family. One must be empathic, sensitive, and inventive to make this relationship constructive. It is important to recognize, however, that understanding and helping the family is an ongoing process of learning and sharing in a context of trust and respect.

The birth of a handicapped child often begins a time of intense spiritual stock taking and soul searching. The pastor can participate in this process and help the family understand and accept what is unchangeable in the handicapping condition while moving beyond those limits in their spiritual life. The pastor's role may be to help the family achieve a philosophical-theological understanding which can provide a foundation for the psychiatric, legal, or societal views which they may encounter.

While there will usually be a need for a number of professional people to be involved with the child and family the pastor has a specific and unique role to play. Most pastors will, in fact, play several roles with the family. Some may arise from the fact that he or she may be a well-established citizen with influence on community agencies and boards; in such a case, the pastor will probably be knowledgeable about available services and can serve as a source for referrals. He or she may also influence social policy and give some direction to the organization of services in the community for children and families. Some pastors may use members of their congregation as a resource, not only to the counseling family but to the community in responding to needs. The major role or opportunity the pastor has when sought by parents is to help them gain theological perspectives in understanding themselves in relation to their handicapped child. The pastor should not be the community organizer, social worker, special educator or psychiatrist, but the pastor. Some pastors may be tempted to enact all of these other professional roles, but to do so may slight their major area of responsibility and result in functioning outside their area of expertise. This is not to say that in the course of any day you may not make yourself available as a first line mental health worker, legal advisor, social worker or counselor. But in this context you should not settle for any of these roles but move to the specific role of spiritual advisor and counselor.

It is important to remember that your credentials are first and foremost those of a minister, and your responsibility is to put matters in a theological perspective. Other perspectives and skills you may have, such as in-depth training in pastoral care of psychology, may assist you, but the dominant frame of reference should be theological. The family will expect that the content of their problem, that of having a handicapped child, will be put in a spiritual perspective by the pastor. This means that many of the unresolved spiritual conflicts or experiences existing between parents may be confronted in the context of their understanding the implications of having a handicapped child.

Your pursuit of the spiritual content of the experience will help form a theological context for the interactions that will occur during the process of helping. A moral or religious self-evaluation on the part of the family may occur and clarification of their beliefs may result. The greatest challenge will be to be available and allow parents to question and clarify theological understandings with the intent of developing deeper spiritual insights. All too often we may be uncomfortable with such pursuits and feel the need to preach or give directions as to what we believe they ought to do. We should assist them in developing their own perspective. When parents turn to you, it is an indication that they want your perspective and they have some theological understandings that may need clarification. They are under stress and are searching for answers that may be inherent in their belief system.

Parents also may want to confess to conflicts and differences and perhaps to lay bare some secrets that have affected their relationship. This experience may expose their anguish and they may need consolation and help in dealing with feelings of despair. They may possess unhealthy attitudes with which they want to be confronted or they may need to be held responsible as parents. They may need the encouragement that is so values in parishioner pastoral relationships, or they may need to be admonished or even rebuked. They may need to be blessed.

The family has a right to expect some specific ministries. No one else will do it for them. A partnership must be established between you and the family. Such partnership will involve mutual expectations for coming together to engage in the process of problem solving. As a professional person you try to look at people and situations in a theological and ethical perspective, undergirded by knowledge and skills which have been assimilated into your pastoral framework of thought and operation.

Most pastors work in churches. Very few do independent work. Thus you represent a specific organization with a particular and specific function to be served. The family before you is faced with a specific event in their life, and they are attempting to deal with a change. The question, then, is how can you serve in facilitating a change and new adaptations.

The needs of the family as a whole are important and should be kept clearly in focus. This is true even whether you minister just to the father or mother or to both of them separately. They cannot be ministered to outside the context of what is good for the handicapped child and the other children in the family. The family is affected both by internal factors such as personality similarities and differences and by external cultural and social factors. All of these come into focus in the counseling process.

The pastor's focus should be to maintain positive and productive relationships and to shift the balance of unproductive interactions among family members so that new forms of relating become possible. If the members wish to be productive as a family, they must be able to support one another in meeting the needs and requirements of productive family life. Families often need help and support in doing this, a need to which pastors in many instances can respond. The pastor can identify roles played by each family member and support the nurturing roles played by certain family members. You will want to be sure that there is an ongoing development of all members in the family. It is important to help create and maintain the avenues for discussion of individual feelings and ideas. One objective you may have in working with the family is to help them to achieve honest, direct communications among themselves about what has happened to them and its theological implications.

A plan must be realistic in nature and must be directly related to the problems identified during your initial interviews. The plan of help is intended to bring about an improved state of spiritual functioning that is transferable outside of the relationship that the family has with you and into all areas of their life. It is a dynamic process, always changing as the result of their personal growth and the new information that becomes available to them and to you during the counseling process.

Remember that one reason the family has come to see you, or that you sought them out, was to attempt to give life to their religious beliefs. Sometimes the best way to accomplish this shared belief is for the family to feel spiritual kinship with you as they seek your help. You can share the fact that before God all people have needs. They may have a shared experience of faith, and there may be a good deal of shared feelings and understanding. Your perspective can be a source of support and renewal of their faith. Praying together occurs in a context of recognizing shared needs.

It is often difficult for individuals to accept and use help. Keith-Lucas points out that "most people do not want to be helped in any significant way. The great majority even of those who ask for help are at the same time very much afraid of it. They may, in fact, actively work to render it fruitless at the same time they ask for it." (Keith-Lucas, page 20). He reminds us that asking for help brings certain demands with it.

Help that makes a difference requires four things. One is that there be some recognition that something is wrong or lacking in a situation and that it cannot be handled alone. The second is that there must be a willingness to tell someone else about the problem. The third is that those in need must be willing to let someone assist them. Fourth, they must be willing to change in some way within themselves. His observations serve to remind us of how very difficult it often is for the family to accept help even when it is desperately needed and sought.

Keith-Lucas also observes that we can expect someone in an encounter with any threatening reality to react in one of four ways: (1) the person may accept and use the threat constructively; (2) he or she may struggle against the reality and try to change it to something else, or (3) try to ward it off by escaping into fantasy or rationalization; or (4) the person may be crushed or paralyzed by the reality. (Keith-Lucas, page 31). Since so much is at stake, the challenge is to help the family move to a constructive use of reality. You cannot remove hurt but you can develop a helping partnership that will lead to a sense of direction and purpose. If that can occur, the hurt will take its place in the human experience of being a family and healthy efforts to cope will occur.

THE PASTOR AS PARACLETE

The concept of advocacy which has evolved in the last few years is important in the role of the pastor. The appropriate Greek word is *paraclete*. It means one who is called alongside of another in order to help. While the major role and function of the pastor is that of proclaiming, it is also essential that he or she fill the function of the paraclete, remaining at the side of individual congregation members and offering what help he or she can. It is also important to move others to be with those who need the help of caring people.

The church is a living and vital system which must perform many functions if it is to continue to meet the definition of the church as a caring community. The well-being of those who constitute the community is essential to the continuance and maintenance of the community. Caring for those needs will take constructive and identifiable form. A measure of the church's vitality may be gained by an examination of what it does for its membership. It is also a measure of how needs have been articulated by the church leadership.

Attempting to understand the role of the paraclete and how it is viewed relative to the needs of the handicapped, the author asked a small group of parents of handicapped children what the church should do for their children.* The parents indicated there is a minimum response from churches to their needs.

As indicated elsewhere, the handicapped child and his or her family pass through several developmental stages, each of which presents a distinct set of difficulties and challenges (see chapter 3).

Parents were asked to describe ways in which the church responded helpfully at each stage of development, and to suggest ways it could improve its responses. One parent's answer is presented here:

> At birth the church could help the parents deal with the guilt and fear that overcomes them. Each one blames the other. This needs to be dealt with. If the church is aware of services offered for the handicapped they could inform the parents. Visiting and offering help to the parents would be greatly appreciated. This is a time when parents feel different and want to withdraw from their friends. Being made to feel that they are loved, not pitied, and included in functions, and so forth, would help them deal with the guilt and fear. Ministers could also offer counseling services to parents to help them in their own relationship with each other, the child and others. Parents need help at this time.
>
> Another important thing the church could do would be to help educate people, the congregation, about handicapped people. Handicapped people do exist. I know that at our church last year on Mental Retardation Sunday, nothing was mentioned in our Sunday School class or during the church services. They had placed flyers inside the bulletin and that was the extent of it. People need to be educated about mental retardation and the church would be an excellent starting place. My husband has made the comment that he would like to hear one sermon a year on people who are different in our society.

Another parent stated:

> Our church has a different person in the nursery each Sunday. Because my child is difficult to manage, it would be better if the same person could

---

*The responses of a small group of parents are reported here because of the value of their ideas and the personal quality of their views. There is no assumption intended that they represent the experiences of most parents or that the churches they describe are necessarily typical.

take the nursery each Sunday. I hate to have to go and explain his condition and behavior each Sunday. Therefore, I just stay home. I have become a hermit because my child's behavior is not socially acceptable.

Parents generally felt that at the time of birth there should be some immediate contact from the church. Some felt they needed counseling, as did the mother quoted previously, and others felt that the pastor and the congregation could help them get in contact with appropriate services in the community.

Many reported that there were no specific and appropriate services being provided by the church. They generally felt excluded and felt that their children were excluded. They thought that ministers were uncomfortable around handicapped people and few people in the church seemed prepared to include their children in church programming. One mother stated, "Most churches just have nurseries but there are not many people who know how to work with the handicapped." One father indicated that the churches that did offer Sunday School programs were dependent on the interest and abilities of no more than one or two people. There was no significant church programming but rather programming by interested individuals. He stated that, "Some teachers will help them, but there again it must be a total program approved by the Church Board." He added, "They are not doing what they should." This same father felt that there should be specific training for teachers and other officials of the church and concluded by saying "if you do not have a loved one that has a problem then usually you will not care. They have a life to live to the fullest also." The parents generally indicated that their needs were most specific and definitive from birth through the early school years. Following that the needs of the handicapped became more obvious in the community and special programs in the community were more helpful.

It was interesting to note that more than one parent indicated that she or he felt that the advocacy or paraclete role of the church and its minister did not end in the church. One mother said, "The church needs to become more vocal and active in advocacy for the handicapped, in awareness of the needs of the handicapped and their families and in making the community aware." She also felt that the church "should be involved in providing for all people who have needs to be loved, to be useful, to have recreation, to have a chance for socialization, to find meaningful activity or occupations, and to have financial security. Handicapped people are no different from nonhandicapped people in their needs except that they have some needs over and above those experienced by 'normal people.'"

THE PASTOR IN THE COMMUNITY

Parents feel the paraclete or advocacy role must be expressed in the larger community for a total environment of caring to exist. The pastor is viewed in most communities as an opinion maker. He or she does have a public forum, the pulpit, and does influence the larger community in its programming for people with special needs. In that role, he or she must have some understanding of the community and its social, political, and bureaucratic structure. He or she should know how important decisions are made and who participates in those decisions. The pastor must be willing to assume some community-wide responsibilities and to have a voice in community affairs if the pastor wants to influence decision makers to respond positively to pastoral concerns on behalf of the church community.

In some ways the needs of communities are a bottomless pit. The more that is accomplished, the more there is to do. Once the pastor has some success as a community advocate, there will be more opportunities to serve. There are usually two broad terms used to capture the essence of the growth of communities: community development and community organization. While there are no widely accepted definitions of either of these terms, they usually involve community work, social planning, community planning, community action, and locality development. Communities may hire professionals to direct some or all of these activities. The size of the community may influence the form taken. Large communities can afford paid professionals to develop formal reports and recommendations for policy making bodys' action, while small communities may have to depend more on informal or softer information systems that may lead decision makers to action. The pastor must know how communities process formal and informal information that leads to decisions if the pastor is to be a successful advocate or paraclete for parents and children.

The pastor may become involved in a wide variety of social issues. These may include welfare reforms, civil rights, education and health issues, meeting the needs of the handicapped or how liquor will be served. There is no end to the possibilities, but in most cases they should be pursued in concert with the pastor's role in a specific congregation. It is risky to attempt to play the role of "community-organizer-at-large." The pastor must have the sanction of a congregation and their involvement in order to succeed in a community role.

The pastor must be prepared to play at least five main roles related to active community involvement. One is that of enabler. For church families this may be one of the most important roles that you as the pastor will play in the community. In this role you help families to articulate their needs so that communities will be led to develop capacities to deal with the problems of their citizens. You may help the parents of the handicapped find others, not only in their own church but perhaps in other churches, who have similar problems. Your role may be that of facilitating an organizational process that will focus the needs, energy and possible discontent of parents and child advocates.

Raising questions which stimulate the development of answers and facilitating the leadership of other people can be very helpful. You may offer encouragement and support without necessarily accepting the responsibility for organizing and directing the action.

The second important role for the pastor in the community is that of broker. People tend to identify you as someone who knows the community and who has the ability to get things accomplished. In the broker role you help individuals and groups who need help but who may not know where help is available in their community. Even moderate-size communities may have in excess of a hundred social service agencies or organizations that provide services. This can be a confusing array of services even to professionals, let alone families who need immediate help. Once a service has been targeted, the broker may help in negotiating the complex network of hurdles to secure the desired service.

A third function or role you must consider is that of expert. Your role is to provide information and direct advice in the area in which you can speak as an authority. In this sense you should not think of the more traditional or limited role of pastor of a congregation, but in terms of the development of a wholesome community. Most pastors have a great deal of understanding about families and their needs. They know a great deal about the organization of the church and its contribution to the larger community. As a pastor of a local congregation, you are in a position to represent a large group of people with common needs in a way that may influence the design and development of community resources.

A fourth role that you can fill in the community is that of planner. You may actively participate in gathering facts about social problems and assist in analyzing those facts so that a course of direction can be planned. You may even participate in seeking funding for such efforts and may play a vital role in securing consensus among diverse interest groups. Once a plan has been developed, you may wish to take some responsibility for its implementation in the community and for securing the support of your congregation. In your planner role you may accept some specific tasks that may lead to developing and implementing programs.

Another role that was discussed earlier is that of advocate or paraclete. If you succeed in diagnosing and interpreting the needs of particular congregation members and suggest some outside or community resource to them, then you obviously must support the process of securing those services. There are times when you will not readily find a match between what is available and the needs you have identified. In your advocate role, you may find yourself in a position of having to challenge institutional or agency indifference to those needs. You must indeed be with your congregation members as they seek help while attempting, if possible, to avoid an adversarial role in the community and its social institutions.

A fifth role that must occasionally be played is that of activist. There are those times when the institutional forms of service are inadequate, nonexistent or in need of change. You must be concerned about injustice, inequity, and barriers to services to families. Families sometimes need help organizing to meet the needs of their children and in some cases assistance in identifying the conflict between those needs and existing services. Such efforts may include negotiation, and even sometimes confrontation and conflict. This can become an uncomfortable role and is one that is usually taken after all else has failed.

It is important to understand that you may assume any one of these roles, but the one involving the least conflict and potential for offending and antagonizing others is the preferred one. It is very important as well to be clear in your own mind about the role you play at any one time and to be as knowledgeable about the demands of such a role as possible.

CONCLUSION

In an ideally just and healthily functioning community, families with handicapped children should be able to look for support to friends and neighbors, their pastor, members of the church congregation, and to the organizations and agencies of the wider community. In terms of our own responsibilities, it is disturbing that many and perhaps most families do not find the church to be a dependable source of help. Yet most churches are quite capable of finding significant ways to respond once they have analyzed the strengths and needs of their membership. However, the church is not equal to the task of meeting all of the needs of handicapped children and their families and must assume some advocacy role in influencing the larger community in its provision of resources. The minister and the members of the congregation usually have specific and visible roles in communities. They help shape community directions through policy formulation and their influence on policy makers. The advocate or the paraclete is one who pleads another's cause. This pleading must occur not only within the context of the church community but it must occur in the larger community as well.

REFERENCES

Keith-Lucas, Alan. *Giving and Taking Help.* Chapel Hill: University of North Carolina Press, 1972.

Perlman, Helen Harris. *Social Casework: A Problem Solving Process.* Chicago: University of Chicago Press, 1957.

Selected National Organizations
and Agencies for Exceptional Children

ACTION (Foster Grandparents Program), 806 Connecticut Avenue, N.W., Washington, D.C. 20525

Alexander Graham Bell Association for the Deaf, Inc., 3417 Volta Place, N.W., Washington, D.C. 20007

Allergy Association of America, 801 Second Avenue, New York, N.Y. 10017.

American Academy for Cerebral Palsy, University Hospital School, Iowa City, Iowa 52240

American Association for Gifted Children, 15 Gramercy Park, New York, N.Y. 10003

American Association for Health, Physical Education, and Recreation, 1201 16th Street, N.W., Washington, D.C. 20036

American Association on Mental Deficiency, 5201 Connecticut Avenue, N.W., Washington, D.C. 20015

American Association for Rehabilitation Therapy, P.O. Box 93, North Little Rock, Arkansas 72116

American Cancer Society, 219 East 42nd Street, New York, N.Y. 10017

American Civil Liberties Union, Juvenile Rights Project, 22 East 40th Street, New York, N.Y. 10016

American Corrective Therapy Association, Inc., 811 Saint Margaret's Road, Chillicothe, Ohio 45601

American Diabetes Association, 18 East 48th Street, New York, N.Y. 10017

American Epilepsy Society, Department of Neurology, University of Minnesota, Box 341, Mayo Building, Minneapolis, Minnesota 55455

American Foundation for the Blind, 15 West 16th Street, New York, N.Y. 10011

American Heart Association, 44 East 23rd Street, New York, N.Y. 10016

American Lung Association, 1790 Broadway, New York, N.Y. 10019

American Occupational Therapy Association, 6000 Executive Boulevard, Rockville, Maryland 20852

American Physical Therapy Association, 1156 15th Street, N.W., Washington, D.C. 20005

American Printing House for the Blind, 1839 Frankfort Avenue, Louisville, Kentucky 40206

American Psychological Association, 1200 17th Street, N.W., Washington, D.C. 20036

American Rheumatism Association, 1212 Avenue of the Americas, New York, N.Y. 10036

American Speech-Language-Hearing Association, 10801 Rockville Pike, Rockville, Maryland 20852

Arthritis Foundation, 1212 Avenue of the Americas, New York, N.Y. 10036

Association for Children with Learning Disabilities, 4156 Library Road, Pittsburgh, Pennsylvania 15234

Association for Education of the Visually Handicapped, 919 Walnut Street, Philadelphia, Pennsylvania 19107

Association for the Gifted of the Council for Exceptional Children, 1920 Association Drive, Reston, Virginia 22091

Association for Severely Handicapped, 1600 West Armory Way, Gardenview Suite, Seattle, Washington 98119

Bureau for Education of the Handicapped, 400 6th Street, Donohoe Building, Washington, D.C. 20202

Call for Action, 575 Lexington Avenue, New York, N.Y. 10022

Center for Sickle Cell Anemia, College of Medicine, Howard University, 520 W Street, N.W., Washington, D.C. 20001

Council for Children with Behavior Disorders of the Council for Exceptional Children, 1920 Association Drive, Reston, Virginia 22091

Easter Seal Society for Crippled Children and Adults, 2023 West Ogden Avenue, Chicago, Illinois 60612

Epilepsy Foundation of America, 1828 L Street, N.W., Suite 406, Washington, D.C. 20036

Goodwill Industries of America, 9200 Wisconsin Avenue, Washington, D.C. 20014

Hemophilia Research, Inc., 30 Broad Street, New York, N.Y. 10004

John Tracy Clinic (Hearing Impairment), 806 West Adams Boulevard, Los Angeles, California 90007

Library of Congress (Division for the Blind and Physically Handicapped), 1291 Taylor Street, N.W., Washington, D.C. 20542

Mental Health Law Project, 1220 19th Street, N.W., Washington, D.C. 20036

Muscular Dystrophy Association of America, 810 Seventh Avenue, New York, N.Y. 10019

National Amputee Foundation, 12–45 150th Street, Whitestone, N.Y. 11357

National Association for Hearing and Speech Action, 10801 Rockville Pike, Rockville, Maryland 20852

National Association for Mental Health, Suite 1300, 10 Columbus Circle, New York, N.Y. 10019

National Association for Music Therapy, Inc., Box 610, Lawrence, Kansas 66044

National Association for Retarded Citizens, 2709 Avenue E East, P.O. Box 6109, Arlington, Texas 76011

National Association of Social Workers, 2 Park Avenue, New York, N.Y. 10016

National Cancer Foundation, 1 Park Avenue, New York, N.Y. 10016

National Center for Law and the Handicapped, Inc., 1235 North Eddy Street, South Bend, Indiana 46617

National Cystic Fibrosis Research Foundation, 3379 Peachtree Road, N.E., Atlanta, Georgia 30326

National Foundation — March of Dimes, 1275 Mamaroneck Avenue, White Plains, N.Y. 10605

National Hemophilia Foundation, 25 West 39th Street, New York, N.Y. 10018

National Institute of Arthritis and Metabolic Disease, Bethesda, Maryland 20014

National Institutes of Health, U.S. Department of Health, Education, and Welfare, Washington, D.C. 20006

National Kidney Foundation, 116 East 27th Street, New York, N.Y. 10016

National Multiple Sclerosis Society, 257 Park Avenue South, New York, N.Y. 10010

National Therapeutic Recreation Society, 1700 Pennsylvania Avenue, N.W., Washington, D.C. 20006

National Society for Autistic Children, 621 Central Avenue, Albany, N.Y. 12206

Registry of Interpreters for the Deaf, P.O. Box 1339, Washington, D.C. 20013

Society for the Rehabilitation of the Facially Disfigured, 500 First Avenue, New York, N.Y. 10016

State Crippled Children Services, Bureau of Community Health Services, 5600 Fishers Lane, Rockville, Maryland 20850

United Cerebral Palsy Association, 66 East 34th Street, New York, N.Y. 10016

United Epilepsy Association, 111 West 57th Street, New York, N.Y. 10019

Viota Speech Association for the Deaf, 1537 35th Street, N.W., Washington, D.C. 20007

The Whole Person, Inc., 9805 Pennsylvania Avenue, Kansas City, Missouri 64114

THE EXCEPTIONAL CHILD

was composed in 10-point VIP Primer and leaded two points
by Partners Composition,
with display type in Bulmer by Dix Typographers, Inc.;
printed on 50-pound acid-free Glatfelter Antique Cream,
Smythe-sewn, and bound over boards in Joanna Arrestox C,
also adhesive-bound with paper covers,
by Maple-Vail Book Manufacturing Group, Inc.;
and published by

SYRACUSE UNIVERSITY PRESS

SYRACUSE, NEW YORK 13210